Also by
Joan Callaway

The Color Connection: From a Retailer's Perspective
It's an Ill Wind, Indeed...that Blows No Good
Invisible to the Eye

Voices

A Collection of Memoirs

SELECTED BY

JOAN CALLAWAY

CONTENTS

VOICES

University Retirement Community Photo by Wes Yates

FOREWORD

Voices. I sent this one-word prompt in an e-mail to the writing group the day I suggested we put together a 'recital' of memoirs written and shared in the writing group of University Retirement Community in Davis, California. I asked each participant to write about a memory or thought the word *Voices* evoked – 50 words or more.

The following Wednesday, the readings in our group ranged from Gailen Keeling's exact fifty words about his parents' voices to Judy Wydick's 550 word memory of a special moment in time with the Davis High School Madrigal singers atop a mesa. Elli Norris used her poetic voice in The Time Machine. Alouise Hillier recalled an angry voice.

Memoirs can begin anytime, anywhere. They can be as brief or as long as you like. They can be simple or complex vignettes of experiences you'd like to share. When I began to write my memoirs, I didn't imagine the journey I would take. To write a memoir means wrestling with the truth. It means you have to travel back in time. Memoir has the power to reveal deep secrets and to expose long-buried thoughts, feelings, and events. It is to whisper your deeply hidden truths, your pain, or your anger, as well as your joy.

Writing memoir takes courage. "What will people think?" "What about my life would be of interest?" "Am I enough?" Staying vulnerable is a risk we have to take if we want to experience connection. Vulnerability is having the courage to show up and be seen. Some say being vulnerable feels dangerous and scary. It may be all of those things, but not nearly as scary as getting to the end of our lives and wondering what if I had dared to write my story.

Sharing our stories in writing group – and now in this year-end 'recital' book for our friends and family – is a most powerful source of connection. Enjoy!

Joan Callaway

Between our first and third Wednesday meetings a month, facilitator Joan Callaway frequently sends a prompt by e-mail. This short piece is the result of such a prompt: Write in 50 words whatever the word 'Voices' evokes.

Prompt – "Voices" and what it evokes in 50 Words[1]

By Gailen Keeling

Dad had a strong baritone voice that commanded attention and authority. Mom had an alto, gentle, teaching-style voice. Their voices made me feel secure, ready to learn and brought stability to what could have developed into chaos among my four siblings and me.

A Note of clarification about my childhood memories:
It would be a stretch of credibility if I remembered all of the details of these events. I remember some of them clearly; others I remember only sketchy outlines. Family members came to my rescue. At reunions and in private conversations, Dad recalled the changes in his life and the moves we made. Mom remembered many of the details about my childhood. Joanna, Bill and Roland helped me recreate events involving them. Thank you, family members, for the details that enrich my life. I encourage everyone who reads my story to write down their own history. Your children, grandchildren and beyond, like mine, will enjoy them, too.

Gailen Keeling

---

[1] Copyright©2014 Gailen Keeling

Davis High School Madrigal Singers   1984-85

VOICES[2]

By Judy Wydick

It was May 1985 when another mother and I chaperoned the twenty-four Davis High School Madrigals on their singing performance tour of Arizona and New Mexico. Dick Luna, owner of DeLuna Jewelry in Davis, which features Native American jewelry and art, had said we really must visit Walpi, an ancient village on top of First Mesa. We arranged our visit after concerts at the Tuba City High School and at the rim of the Grand Canyon.

The long, narrow mesa stands three hundred feet high and contains three small, primitive villages: the original Old Walpi, farthest from the entrance at the top of the mesa (established about 900 AD, now deserted); the middle village (which split off from the original before 1600), and the first village (descendants of a more fierce tribe, invited after the 1640 revolt to live near the entrance to protect the inner villages from soldiers). Tall, feathered sticks, carefully placed, indicate the boundaries of each.

We wandered through the first two villages, stopping occasionally where people were selling wares, then past the ruins of Old Walpi. Gradually the Madrigals collected at the far end of the mesa in a wide, open area—completely, grandly *open.* We could see forever!

Aside from our being so high up, what made this place so special? The magnificent billowing clouds against the blue Arizona sky? The rugged barrenness, the absence of man-made structures as far as we could see? The gentle breeze, the absolute quiet, the muted colors everywhere except for the bits of wild grass struggling through the rocks beneath our feet?

The students themselves were quiet, some sitting on boulders, others talking softly or simply gazing at the distant natural monuments. And suddenly I knew we needed more—their music to bring it all together. I said they simply had to sing *Shenendoah,* that haunting ballad

---

7

that was part of their repertoire. "But why, Mrs. Wydick?" "Just do it," I said. "You'll understand when you do it."

Malcolm Mackenzie (age 15 then, now long a professional opera singer), set the tone in his rich bass-baritone, and was quickly joined by the others singing the first verse in unison. And starting with the second verse, they separated into rich four-part harmony, supported by the deep basses. The ballad may have originated in the soft, tree-covered hills and valleys of Virginia, but the nostalgic sounds of yearning were perfect for the moment.

Oh Shenandoah,
I long to see you,
Away you rollin' river.
Oh Shenandoah,
I long to hear you,
Away, I'm bound away,
'Cross the wide Missouri.

Oh Shenandoah,
I long to see you,
Away you rollin' river.
Oh Shenandoah,
I long to hear you,
Away, I'm bound away,
'Cross the wide Missouri.

Oh Shenandoah,
I'm bound to leave you,
Away you rollin' river.
Oh Shenandoah,
I'll not deceive you,
Away, I'm bound away,
'Cross the wide Missouri.

Some say this early American folk song is about a trader's love of the daughter of the Indian chief, Shenandoah. And what did the Hopi villagers think when they heard this beautiful melody drifting into their lives, so separate from the rest of the world? I'd like to think they felt it was a thank you for allowing us to experience their mesa. I know none of us there that day will ever forget it.

We could see forever!

We All Live in a Wondrous Time Machine...[3]

By Elli Norris

I've been traveling in this time machine for 80 years and some weeks, and I'm still discovering times and places I'd forgotten existed. Furthermore, I'm realizing that, under the right circumstances, I can travel in other people's time machines, too.

For example, just the other day I watched a little girl sitting on her father's lap in front of me at a concert, walking her fingers up and down the top of the seat before her. Playing the piano?

Watching her sweet, pudgy little hands suddenly transported me back 70 years and I, too, am a sweet little girl, maybe 5 or 6 years old. I have fallen asleep in the back seat of the old maroon Ford as our family drives the dauntingly windy Ridge Route from our temporary home in Los Angeles to Porterville. We are on the way to Grandma and Grandpa's house for Christmas. My journey back in time doesn't bring forth the ride itself, only the part where I rise enough out of the depths of sleep to know I am lying safe in my father's arms as he carries me from the back seat into Grandma's house and to bed. Oh, sweet memory.

I made several other Time Machine voyages recently with a long-time friend whom I was visiting in Colorado. Peggy and I have been friends for nearly 50 years, and as we relived old times (and created many new ones) we revisited Palo Alto, Ann Arbor, Laramie, Boulder, and now Longmont, Colorado, not to mention Berkeley, my family ranch in Tulare County, and Santa Barbara and Davis. We saw ourselves in our 20s and 30s and...and...and now. Oh, the travels through time and space we made together! She let me visit some of the time places in her Time Machine, too, and I took her with me to some of my memory places. Life, we agreed, is a roller-coaster, a trip, a banquet, a Time Machine!

---

[3]Copyright©2014 Eleanor L. Norris

When I moved into the University Retirement Community in December of 2011, I didn't comprehend at first that I was moving into a Time Machine. Yet I soon learned, as I sat at dinner with newly-met people, that each one of them could take me to times and places I never knew.

Then I discovered the book of biographies of URC residents which resides in the swimming pool lounge. I leaved through its pages and traveled from the early 1920s to the Great Depression, to World War II and the Korean Conflict, and all the years in between and afterward. Traveled, too, from Sofia, Bulgaria to Prague, Czechoslovakia, to Indonesia, India, Hong Kong, Egypt, Spain, England, Palestine under the British mandate, and more. And, of course, small towns in the Midwest, the U.S. north and south and east and west, and Davis, California.

Here's another trip I took just the other day, back to the '60s (the 1960s, of course). As I traveled in my Time Machine, voices so familiar came into my ears and I knew it was...the Beatles, singing this song. "We all live in a yellow submarine, yellow submarine, yellow submarine." And then I heard in my own mind's ear, "We all live in a wondrous Time Machine, wondrous Time Machine, wondrous Time Machine..."

That's a song I can just keep on singing, now and...onward.

A PAINFUL LESSON[4]

By *Alouise Hillier*

"Can't you EVER do anything right?!"
The uncharacteristic angry outburst
   from beloved Aunt Ann
   shocked and hurt me deeply.

Admittedly, I had been careless
   when I measured and marked
   the hemline of her dress under construction.

I determined that I never again wanted
   to hear such a comment.
I would do *something* well, but what?

From early childhood I had enjoyed sewing.
I determined to BE THE BEST
   in every project I made.

Aunt Ann's unkind words proved to be
   a valuable lesson to me.
She would be favorably impressed
   to see Best of Show and Sweepstakes ribbons
   hanging in my sewing room.

Alouise Hillier's Best of Show Quilt

GAILEN'S MORAL DILEMMA
WATERMELONS ALONG THE RAILROAD[56]
TRACK

By Gailen Keeling

My friend's big Buick stopped a short distance from the railroad crossing. Three of my friends from the football team and I stepped out of the car onto the graveled shoulder of the road. We headed toward the crossing. When we reached the tracks, the four of us turned east toward our target, a large field of ripe watermelons. Running on the railroad ties, we arrived in just a few minutes.

Time was of the essence. Mr. McGregor had two large dogs. We heard them barking in the distance. They were the protectors of this 10 acre patch of melons. One boy had wire cutters and made a small opening in the barbed-wire fence.

Each of us tapped a large melon, listening for the sound that assured they were ripe, and lifted them to our shoulders. We ran back through the opening in the barbed-wire fence.

A quick sprint down the tracks to the car parked 100 yards away was an easy trip for this quartet, except for one boy. His watermelon slipped from his shoulder, busted as it hit the end of a railroad tie and rolled down the gravel embankment that supported the track. The three melons that remained were laid in the back seat, plenty of ripe fruit for four.

With sighs of relief, we drove to the high school. We sat on the high curb that lined the street in front of the high school - eating our

---

bounty. A police car patrolling the adjacent neighborhood, slowly approached us and stopped.

The young officer looked out his window. "Where did you steal those melons?" he asked.

The only senior among us replied, "From farmer McGregor's field. He has so many, he'll never miss them." As he drove closer, we saw him clearly in the street light. He had been the star fullback of the football team that had won the league championship six years ago. He paused a few minutes. As we sat on the curb, we began to sweat. What will he do?

The officer spoke in a firm voice, "You have disgraced the school, and you took a big risk. Clean up this mess and go home."

We gathered up the rinds and got into the car. Because I lived nearby, they drove me home first.

Everyone at my house was asleep. I went to my room and sat on my bed thinking, "What am I going to do?" I had done something wrong. Stealing the melons was wrong. What do I do? No one may ever find out what we did. But, what if one of the boys tells others and they spread what we did? What if the police officer reported us? What if the school principal finds out? What if my parents find out - what would they do?

That night, restful sleep did not rescue me. I kept turning and tossing. I was thinking -What am I going to do? No answer came to me. If I told Dad, he would probably report it to the Police Chief who would tell Principle Stevens. The other boys would get in trouble along with me. They would think I had ratted on them. What am I going to do?

Our family tradition was to go to church on Sunday. As I dressed for church, I decided to bite the bullet and tell Dad what I had done. I called for him to come to my room. After a few minutes, his large frame appeared in the door.

"Dad, I did something very wrong last night and I knew it was wrong. He sat down beside me. As I began telling the events of the night before, I tried hard not to cry, but my emotions overtook me.

16

Slowly the tears began rolling down my cheek and I stopped talking. Dad broke the silence.

"Gailen, you made a big mistake. I must call the police and Mr. McGregor. Come downstairs with me while I make the calls." Dad told the Police Chief everything. The Chief told Dad that he knew of the incident. The young officer did his duty. He wrote up the incident in his log book. The officer told the Chief that he did not arrest anyone or give a citation, because he had not witnessed the event. He had not observed a crime. The Chief told Dad that he would call Principal Stevens and Mr. McGregor.

On Monday morning, before class started, Mr. Stevens called the four of us into his office. When we arrived, he took us into the conference room adjacent to his office. As we entered the room, I was shocked at what I saw. Around the large table sat the Police Chief, the young officer, Mr. McGregor and six parents, including Dad. Mr. Stevens asked the Chief to speak first.

"Young men," he began. "You have done something that is very serious, stealing property and trespassing. These are Class C felonies. If charged and convicted, you would not go to jail. The law provides for parole and supervision, requires the convicted to make restitution. It would be a public record that could appear on your school records. Because you have potential to become positive and productive young men, I am taking Mr. Keeling's recommendation that you not be charged with a crime. Instead, I am turning your punishment over to Mr. Stevens and Mr. McGregor, and your parents.

Mr. Stevens stood up and asked the four of us to stand. "We paint the stadium bleachers every three years. This is the year. This will be the job for the four of you. You will work with the Janitor and his assistant in painting them. You will also help him move the furniture back into the classrooms from the gym where they have been taken for repair" After a few minutes, he then asked, "Mr. McGregor would you like to speak?"

"Yes I would, Mr. Stevens. I played on the football team 20 years ago. I consider every team my team. I do not want these young men to be suspended from the team, not even for one game. I want to see them out there every game working their butts off, excuse my language, helping our team get another victory."

"As for the damage you did," he continued, "the fence you cut and the melons you took, I want to be compensated for my time repairing the fence and the cost of the melons. It will be a total of $40, or $10 each."

Mr. Stevens then addressed the parents: "I believe what we heard is adequate punishment for what your sons have done. However you have the prerogative to use your best judgment in this matter."

My Dad did not punish me further. Following a talk with Mom, each week I drove out to Mr. McGregor's fruit-stand and bought a ripe water melon and paid for it with my own money.

Dilemma resolved.

The Keeling Family L-R Roland, Joanna, Dad, Jay, Bill, Me and Mom

ON HUMOR

Lisa Tener, Book Writing Coach: *It seems to me that humor is a factor in all the bestsellers from Eat Pray Love to Running with Scissors to The Glass Castle. Especially when writing about the horrific, these authors transport us with humor. Why do you think humor is important in memoir?**

Greg Miller, Author: *Three reasons:*

One is the same reason many horror movies include laughs. A laugh releases tension that would otherwise become genuinely unpleasant if it continued uninterrupted.

Two, humor creates dynamics and introduces another color and dimension to a story.

Three, humor signifies authenticity. If you can laugh at yourself, it tells an audience you know yourself and that's reassuring. It enhances your credibility.

*From an interview: http://www.lisatener.com/2010/08/dry-memoir-get-serious-about-being-funny/

IT WAS THE CAT'S FAULT[7]
or
WHY WE HAD TO BUY A DISHWASHER AND REFRIGERATOR AT THE SAME TIME
By Judy Wydick

Anyone who has lived in Davis is aware of the rat problem. Often at night you can see them running along the fence. From time to time, our cat Lucille brought us four-legged gifts through the dog door. I'm not aware that she ever actually killed one, probably because she was never that hungry.

For example, once during dinner, having dashed into the dark dining room to speak on the phone, I discerned Lucille's distinctive mouth-full cry and quickly turned on the light. Startled, she dropped a rat at my feet; and Dick, reacting to my screech, raced to my rescue. (Actually, he simply picked up the phone off the floor to explain to our son that I had left to chase a rat.)

Our German shepherd Greta, hearing the commotion, rushed to do her part, and between us, we worked the creature around the living room until it ran out the front door that I had opened just in time. Peering into the darkness, I could see it running down the sidewalk and across the street, where it scurried up a driveway and into my neighbor's garage. Oh well . . .

On the occasion about which I am writing, however, I was alerted by the painter in our kitchen that we had a rat there: it had run over his foot when he moved the refrigerator. Of course we knew why: Lucille had brought it in to play with, and it had gotten away.

It had been a while since Dick had replenished the poisoned grain in his carefully-designed apparatus outside. Too long, apparently. And this rat had taken up housekeeping under the refrigerator. With the cat's bowls of dry food and water located just beside it, the rat was obviously comfortably situated for the duration.

21

So I quickly called Clark Pest Control to help us out. They said all they could do was dispense poison. Ordinarily, they wouldn't do so when the rat was inside the house; but since it could go out the dog door to get water needed after ingesting the poison, they agreed to come do it as long as I got rid of its food and water supply next to the fridge.

I did, they came, and then we waited. Several days later, a distinctive odor began wafting about the kitchen. We quickly realized the rat had not left the house (perhaps, in his despair, he had forgotten the dog door), so I looked under the fridge, but it wasn't there. Dick thought it might have gotten into the area behind the sink, but it wasn't there either.

So he unscrewed the dishwasher from its moorings and pulled it out to see if it was back behind it. That is when the air turned blue. In so doing, he had broken the copper line through which water enters the dishwasher. Not only was the rat not ensconced back there; whenever we turned on the water in the sink, it poured out onto the floor.

The only place left to look was under the cabinetry. When the carpenters had finished putting together the kitchen, they had placed long, narrow finish-boards under the cabinets, except for one small space where Lucille as a kitten used to run through to hide. We realized it had gone in there, which would place it now anywhere under the cabinets or stove. And Dick, having learned a lesson from pulling out the dishwasher, knew he hadn't the time or talent to remove the boards. So the next day I called Bill Cavins of Ganesh Works (a fix-it shop) who said he'd be right out.

Bill agreed with our assessment of the rat's location. As he began getting out his tools, I decided to use his flashlight to take a last look under the refrigerator—and this time I saw it, caught up in the coils. Bill asked me for a yardstick so he could get it out. But instead, as he pressed, the yardstick went right *through* the rat. If we thought the odor was bad before, *now* it was unbearable.

I called Dick at the law school, as we had to make some quick decisions. We realized that as we had no way to extract the rat, we had to get rid of the refrigerator. Though it worked perfectly, it was 18 years old, so it would soon need to be replaced anyway.

As for the dishwasher, it was new when the house was built 16 years before. It, too, was working fine; but the cost of repair was such that it was better to invest the money in a new one.

So I immediately called Goodwill, who happily sent someone to get the refrigerator (in spite of its current condition), then Pearson's, who were delighted to provide us with two new appliances. By the next day, everything was in place, and the odor had almost disappeared. Everyone was glad we could finally use the kitchen, and I was impressed with the improvements made in the two appliances.

It was not the end of our experiences with rats, however, but it was the most expensive. I'll save those *other* stories for another time.

The Infamous Rat

THE TOILET STORY[8]

By Judy Wydick

I was away in Missouri when Jing, the Chinese scholar living with us, was cleaning the house. His job w as to clean the house once a week, and he was doing it now so it would be ready when I arrived home.

He was just starting to vacuum in our bedroom when he came toward my desk—and saw, protruding from some papers that had fallen there, the long tail of a rat! No one else was in the house, and Jing knew he couldn't just leave it there, but he also didn't want to touch it. So he went down into the garage to find a pair of pliers with which to pick it up. The only ones he could find was a small pair perhaps four inches long, so that had to do. The tail was still there when he returned, so he reached down, pinched the tail in the pliers, and pulled out the rat.

But immediately as he was standing up, the rat began writhing and arching its back to get at what was holding it. Jing, fearing he would be bitten, wildly looked about to see where he could get rid of the rat, when he realized that the closest place was around the corner in the toilet. "So I threw it in the toilet, but it tried to get out, so I grabbed the green *prastical* tuber and pushed it back in; but then it tried to crawl up the *prastical* tuber, so I dropped the tuber and rat and flushed the toilet! The water went up very high, and then it went down very slowly! The rat and the *prastical* tuber are gone, but I know I did something bad to the toilet!"

This is what he said to Dick, whom he called immediately after all this happened. Dick could never understand Jing over the phone in the first place, and now Jing was so frantic that Dick couldn't get a word of what he was saying, except "toilet" and "rat."

"Is this an emergency?" Dick interrupted firmly. "I'm just about to go teach my class. Can it wait until I get home at 4?" Dick said there was a brief pause, but then Jing started trying to explain again. "Tell me what happened when I get home," he said, hoping he had guessed correctly.

As Dick drove up to the house, Jing was waiting anxiously for him out in the yard, hands wringing. He hurriedly took him up to the bathroom, explaining what had happened, and Dick responded that he would call the plumber, and that the plumber would fix it. Not to worry. But of course Jing was beside himself with worry.

By the time the plumber arrived, Dick had figured out that the "*prastical* tuber" Jing had talked about was the green plastic bottle of Ban Deodorant that usually sat in the small bathroom window above the toilet.

The plumber put his cable "snake" down the toilet, twisted it, and brought out one very dead rat; but try as he might, he couldn't remove the Ban bottle. So he had to go out and turn off the water, then empty the water from the toilet, unscrew the toilet from the floor, and lift the whole thing into the bath tub upside down. He could then simply reach in and remove the Ban bottle, after which he did everything in reverse. One hundred and fifty nine dollars later (probably a bargain), everything was in fine shape, and he was on his way, after confessing that he had extracted many interesting items from toilets, but this was a new one.

Jing was still distraught that he had caused so much trouble, but Dick kindly explained that he might have done the same thing himself, that such things happen, and truly, he should no longer worry about it.

Dick told me the whole story that night when he came to pick me up at the airport, and I've rarely ever laughed so hard. I later joined

26

Dick in putting Jing at ease, and by then he could also see a certain humor in what happened.

And I think Jing would also be pleased that this "Toilet Story" and the "Whack Whack Story" are two of my granddaughters' favorites. Only recently they asked me to please write them down. And that is what I remembered to do after I wrote up the "Kitchen Rat Story." One likes to keep one's granddaughters entertained.

Queen Judy

WHEN I WAS A PRINCESS[9]

By Judy Wydick

Once upon a time I was a princess. Really. I told my grand-daughters about it during their Princess phase at five or six, but they didn't believe me. I even showed them pictures, but apparently I didn't fit the profile.

It's true, however. It began the summer I turned 18. One of my mother's friends asked if I would represent AAUW as a contestant for Queen of the Eldon Fair. Eldon, Missouri, a town of about 2,000 inhabitants, was the economic center of the area—where the doctor, dentist, and major businesses were located.

I said I would, and my first memory is of having to go for an interview the day after I had walked through a nest of chiggers that left hundreds of bites on my legs, and I had to wear hose—and probably a girdle. The big event was an appearance in formals the first night of the Eldon Fair. I won and, sitting on the back of a convertible, was driven around the arena by my brother, wearing his best Hawaiian shirt.

Then, as Queen of the Eldon Fair, I became Eldon's entry to compete for Queen of the 1955 American Royal Livestock and Horse Show in Kansas City in early October—after beginning freshman year at the U. of Colorado. Once there, I asked the Dean of Women permission to miss three days of school. I explained that the top three girls selected would also have to remain an extra week to carry out their obligations, but that I certainly wouldn't be one of them. She noted that was a good thing, as anyone missing so many classes might as well not return to school.

So, on the appointed Wednesday, I happily flew off to Kansas City. There I met other college girls from Missouri and the surrounding states, and Thursday we all went through the personal interviews. Such things are great fun when nothing is at stake.

Friday, dressed in our formals, we paraded before the judges, who occasionally questioned us. I was called back several times, which was annoying, because it kept interrupting conversations I was having with other contestants. And no one was more surprised than I when I ended up being selected one of the three—the other princess the Homecoming Queen from Oklahoma State, the queen representing Marshall, Missouri. The queen and I were clearly small town girls, the other princess definitely a beauty.

The three of us had been given gorgeous full ball gowns (mine was pale pink) that cascaded over large bell-shaped hoops. At a gala the next evening in a ballroom, the crowning of the queen was the major event. First, the eight ladies-in-waiting came out, and then I was the first of the two princesses to be presented. Each of us wore a wine-colored velvet cape with a high collar and long train and carried two-dozen long-stemmed red roses.

Upon being announced, I was met by my 28-year-old escort from the Kansas City Junior Chamber of Commerce. We walked down the length of the ballroom to stand on one side of the throne, followed shortly by the other couple, the princess lovely in light green. Then, to great fanfare, came the queen in her white ball gown. She was met by heartthrob singer Eddie Fisher, who escorted her to her throne, where he stood on a box to be tall enough to place her crown. He then led her out to begin the dancing, his new young wife, actress Debbie Reynolds, watching nearby.

Afterwards we were taken to a dinner, and I sat across from Betty Furness (remember her from *What's My Line?*), who had been the master-of-ceremonies that evening. It had taken me so long to get my hoop-filled dress collected as I was seated that I didn't stand when introduced to her, which drew a hard look from my mother: no excuse would do for not standing when introduced to an older woman! (She might have been 40.) One remembers things like that.

I also well remember afterwards when our escorts, who felt they should do something special with us, took us to a nightclub. As we were being seated, right in front, my escort seemed to have second thoughts and muttered something like "Perhaps this wasn't the best choice." Not realizing what was coming, I didn't pay any attention, as we had excellent seats. The entertainment, however, turned out to be strippers, the highlight being a woman who could twirl her breasts singly, together, or in opposite directions, tassels flying wildly. It seemed impolite to look at her, but more so *not* to. Then she seemed to be *performing for my date*, and my only thought was, "If that woman comes over and sits in his lap, I will absolutely *die!*"

Princess Judy on left

But she didn't. It was quite an evening.

Saturday was the American Royal Parade, where we sat on the royal float below the queen. The temperature was in the 20s, so we wore long underwear beneath our gowns and lovely fur coats to cut the wind—a cut above my own mouton coat.

The next seven days were a blur of racing through the streets in a large black car with red flags on the front fenders, led by two policemen on motorcycles—sirens screaming—to attend multiple breakfasts, lunches and dinners. Best were appearances every afternoon and evening at the Horse Show in the main box, seated with whatever dignitaries were there.

Once, hearing a familiar voice behind me, I whirled around blurting, "I know you," when, to my horror, I realized I *didn't!* He introduced himself as "H.V. Kaltenborn," whom we used to hear regularly on the radio!

One day we were all given massages to help us relax, but do you know how much a massage can tickle? Mrs. Russell Stover presented us each with a 10-pound box of chocolates, and someone gave us beautiful Stetson hats. I also have a recording from being on the Dave Garraway Show.

We were photographed at each event, usually with the heads of organizations or well-known political figures. Among the photos we were given are pictures of a lieutenant from the Olatha (Kansas) Naval Base shakily pinning wings on my blouse, of Mr. Hall showing us some Hallmark cards, and of us balanced precariously on the rails beside the prize bull (who kept bumping us and who later sneezed all over the other princess's dress).

The festivities finally over, I returned to Colorado, exhausted but looking forward to telling about it all. My roommate and boyfriend met me at the airport and politely listened for a bit, but they clearly weren't interested. Nor was anyone else. So things quickly returned to normal, which made it easy to get down to studying. I didn't flunk out.

But for a very short time, I really was a princess. Maybe my last grandchild, now four, will believe me. There's always a chance.

Princess Judy on the left

Daisy, A Therapeutic Clown

MY JOURNEY INTO CLOWNING[10]

By Nancy Maynard

Feeling scared, angry and more than a little sorry for myself, I needed cheering up. Still reeling from my doctor's diagnosis of cardiomyopathy, a damaged heart, a heart in need of laughter, Carol and I decided to go to our favorite vacation spot for a little get-away. I wanted some time to get things into perspective.

We headed north to Ephraim where our friends Joan and Walt own a Bed and Breakfast. Sitting in their living room listening to the story of my sad and damaged heart, Joan said, "You need to go to Clown Camp."

CLOWN CAMP!? Now that sounded intriguing, but I could never be a clown. I don't like calling attention to myself. I don't have a great sense of humor. I can occasionally be silly when it comes to playing with children or goofing around with close friends. but being a clown means performing magic tricks, making animals out of balloons, walking in parades and doing slapstick.

I hate slapstick. But the more Joan talked of how much fun she had at the camp and all the funny people she met and how she laughed from morning until night, I knew I had to try it. It didn't mean I had to be a clown. I could just go and laugh. It turns out that Wisconsin has a nationally known clown camp on the state university campus in Stevens Point. This is where Joan went. I sent for the brochure, it came, and I signed up.

The time came and I drove to Stevens Point with the things on the list they said to bring, mostly items for a costume. I wasn't sure about this, so didn't want to put a lot of money or effort into it –a pair of jeans, a red T-shirt, wide multi-colored striped suspenders and a silly beanie hat. That would have to do. I was supposed to have a clown name, but that would just have to wait. I wasn't going to be a clown anyway. I just wanted to laugh.

---

[10] Copyright©2014 Nancy Maynard

Well, laugh I did, but more importantly I met people who quickly became friends. They were so willing and eager to share their humor and encourage a laugh, to lend a piece of clothing to embellish my costume, and to teach me all the tricks of the trade. "Olena" gave me a pair of blue gloves to add to my costume. "Jello" loaned me an over-sized yellow tie with a huge bow and "Tink" put a pair of large glasses on my face and said, "You look great!"

Balloon class & Face painted

I took classes in face painting and making animals with balloons and exaggerating facial expressions. I was not an eager student. Making a fool of myself was uncomfortable. I just wanted to laugh and enjoy. Each person had their own idea about what clowning was and what clowns did. Most felt it was entertaining people, performance cleverly planned and perfectly executed to make themselves look like fools, thus making people laugh. Some did it with silly oversized props. Some did it with magic tricks and some with words. I found all this interesting and, as an audience member, I thoroughly enjoyed it, BUT I didn't want to do it. I am not a performer.

Then at lunch one day I met Korey Thompson. Her idea of clowning was not that of performance, but of simply and deliberately connecting with people. Using her silliness, she reached for each person's spirit. She used no props, no jokes, no magic tricks. She used only herself and her intention to connect.

She told of "clowning" in hospitals and nursing homes, particularly with dementia patients. Now that I could do! As a nurse, I had been doing that my entire career. I could exchange my nursing uniform for a clown suit. Instead of "being there" for people as a nurse/teacher, I could "be there" for people as a clown.

The "treatment" I offer as 'Daisy' is laughter and a way out of isolation, rather than medicine. As I tried it, I discovered that all I had to do was put on my clown face, smile, make eye contact, wave, blow a few bubbles, and people laughed, particularly people with dementia. I found my special place as a clown. My "impaired heart" now brought joy to those with impaired brains.

CHILDHOOD MEMORIES

"Childhood memories were like airplane luggage; no matter how far you were traveling or how long you needed them to last, you were only ever allowed two bags. And while those bags might hold a few hazy recollections—a diner with a jukebox at the table, being pushed on a swing set, the way it felt to be picked up and spun around—it didn't seem enough to last a whole lifetime."—Jennifer E. Smith, *This is What Happy Looks Like*

CHILDHOOD MEMORIES[11]

By Gailen Keeling

FROM BARBER TO BREAD SALESMAN

Dad was a very skilled barber, and he had the personality to go with it. The times that I went downtown and visited him at his shop, I saw that his customers liked him. He had invested a lot in his education and of himself – and he was using it well. He was generous. A beauty shop could not make enough money to locate in the small farming communities, so he offered all of his male customers the opportunity to bring in their wives to get their hair trimmed or shaped without charge. He trimmed long pony tails, cut Boy-Bob haircuts and shaped bangs. Working in rural communities was Dad's favorite location.

In 1934, the depression deepened in Wichita. Grain, flour and beef shipments were no longer going overseas, where the Great Depression was growing. Dad's business was getting slower and slower. He could no longer earn enough money to provide for his family. When he announced that he had stopped barbering, he also told us, "I will never go on welfare, even if I have to work two or three part time jobs."

Dad looked for work. He found a small neighborhood bakery that was planning to expand and go city-wide. They were looking for route salesmen to sell their bread and cookies. He was interested, but he couldn't meet one requirement. You had to have your own truck. We had an old car - no truck.

Miracles do happen. While Dad was searching for work, Mom got the news from her brother, Loren, that she would receive a small

---

inheritance from their parents' estate. Part of it was the value of the family farm that Loren was farming. He decided to keep the farm and give his four sisters their share in money. When Mom received her share, she gave part of the money to Dad for the truck he needed.

Dad came home with a panel truck. I saw painted on its side, "Kitchenette Baking Co. – Bread and Kookies." As I looked at the spelling, I thought, if you are a big company, you don't have to worry about spelling. You could spell words any way you wanted to spell them.

Competition in bakery sales was tough. The owners of the bakery believed they could compete with Wonder Bread, the predominant supplier of bread in the Wichita market. It is the same company you see in the stores today with its bread wrapped in their traditional red, yellow and blue dotted wrapper. It sold for 10 cents a loaf. The owners of the bakery where Dad now worked believed they could put out a quality loaf that the stores could sell for two loaves for 15 cents.

Dad's uniform consisted of a light blue shirt and a black bow tie with yellow polka dots on it. His name was embroidered above the pocket in yellow thread. He wore a light blue cap that resembled the kind I saw railroad switchmen wearing. I remember seeing Dad walk into the house at the end of his workday. He was tall and husky and looked sharp in his uniform. Mom told him that he looked handsome.

Dad needed to sign up many stores to develop his route. He entered a store and introduced himself. He told the owner that he wanted shelf space on the bread and cookie aisle. Dad said, "If you give me the space, I will leave ten loaves of bread, without payment, and return tomorrow to see the results." He also told the owner, "If you decide to sell my bread, you will make as much per loaf as you do selling a loaf of Wonder Bread. I believe that setting the price at two loaves for fifteen cents you will sell more loaves – and make more profit for you and me."

Returning to the store the next day, he often found a happy store owner with all of the bread he had left the previous day sold. Several of the owners told Dad that customers commented, "It tastes like home-made bread and much better than that soft bread." This thrilled Dad. The store now became a regular stop on his daily route.

It took Dad many days to enlist enough stores to build up a large route. He worked long hours, arising very early in the morning before daylight. He came home in the mid-afternoon. The price of the bread being two loaves for fifteen cents, Dad, the bakery, and the store each received two and one half cents per loaf. Delivering and selling hundreds of loaves each day was hard work. After supper, Dad was very tired – and the entire family went to bed early – on "kid time."

Now, the family had more spendable money. From struggling along making $40-$45 a month as a barber, Dad was now earning $70-$75 a month. Mom was pleased because she no longer worried about having the money to pay the $5 weekly rent.

Dad carried a long, leather pouch chained to his belt. When he came home, it was full of coins and a few dollar bills. He had already paid the bakery. What was left was his - to buy gas, maintain the truck, keep a good looking uniform and provide for our family. I saw his face filled with a look of satisfaction. When he greeted Mom, their kisses and hugs lasted longer. Previously, when they talked about money and spending, I felt uneasy. Now, I felt safe and secure.

Dad walked to the kitchen table, drank a cup of coffee that Mom prepared, and did his daily accounting. He took out of his pocket the list of accounts that showed the money he received from each store. With his index finger he went down the column of figures - from top to bottom - and registered the total. Then, he moved his finger to the next column where he repeated his addition to arrive at the total. He did not use an adding machine. He did the calculation only once. Sometimes, Joanna and Bill checked his addition. They found no mistakes. Dad was accurate. All of us children were amazed at his addition skills. I was especially interested because Joanna was teaching me to count.

Then, Dad emptied the money from the leather pouch onto the table. He put it into stacks of pennies, nickels, dimes and quarters. Occasionally, a silver or paper dollar appeared. After

41

counting the money, Dad compared the money with the total from his list of accounts. They were the same. He tapped his pencil a few times on the table, put it down, raised his head and sat back in the chair. A look of satisfaction filled his face.

Roland, Joanna, Bill and Me - 1934

THE BEST TOYS

Roland and I had no store bought toys. We had to make our own. Several houses were being remodeled in our neighborhood. We visited one site and asked the foreman if we could have some of the discarded shingles and wooden pieces. He said we could take as much as we wanted.

When we got home with our loot, we took black and brown crayons and drew doors, headlights, windshields and wheels on the wood. The small pieces were now cars, the longer ones were trucks, and out of the largest pieces of wood we made construction equipment. Now we had toys.

Wannabe engineers that we were, we planned it out. The roads we built wound through the dirt next to the porch, through the grass and weeds, around the trunk of a large tree - ending under the branches and leaves of a mulberry bush. The shingles and 2x4s were our bridges and sidewalks. These toys provided us with hours of fun. The fruits of our labor were reflected in our dirty hands and fingernails.

One Saturday, when we knew we were due for a bath, Roland and I hid under the mulberry bush. We hoped that, if we were out of sight, Mom would forget. Wrong we were. Mom called us.

When we did not respond, she came looking for us. We had thought we were clever. She simply went to the edge of the porch, followed the road through the grass and weeds, around the trunk of the large tree (probably chuckling all the way), and looking into the shadows under the mulberry bush, she found us. There was no punishment. Maybe Mom thought the bath was enough.

THE LITTLE THIEF

When school began in the fall of 1935, I was alone - to play by myself. My fifth birthday was in August. A student needed to be six to enter first grade. My siblings, Joanna, Bill and Roland were back in school. One-year-old Jay Roy was not old enough or big enough to be a meaningful playmate.

It was the first day of school. I needed something to do. I walked down the alley toward the yard of my six-year-old buddy, Fred Good. On many summer days, I traveled this route. I knew that Fred would not be home. He was old enough to be in school.

I approached his house and went through the back gate. Lying there beside the tall concrete barbeque pit was a small, bright red truck. Something to play with," I thought. I picked up the toy - put it in my pocket and headed back home - with the bed of the truck sticking out of the pocket of my coveralls.

Mom was on the back porch finishing the Monday laundry. She saw the bulge in my pocket and the red object sticking out. "What do you have there, Gailen?"

"A red truck."

"Where did you get it?"

"The truck is not yours.

Remember what I have taught? You are not to take things that are not yours. You must return it to Fred's Mom right now!" Mom talked to me in her firm voice. I realized I had broken a family teaching: you do not take anything at any time that does not belong to you. Mom looked disappointed. I felt bad and sad.

I pleaded. "Will you go with me?"

"No, Gailen. You took it alone. You can return it alone."

With watery eyes I walked slowly down the alley - turning - to see if Mom was still there. She was - on the steps of the porch with her hands on her hips - looking in my direction and motioning with her hand and arm for me to continue.

I went through the gate, past the barbeque pit and walked to the back porch. Mrs. Good saw me coming and met me there. "I took Fred's truck. I'm bringing it back," I said in a wobbly voice. Tears rolled gently down my cheeks.

"Thank you, Gailen," she said, as I handed her the truck.

Quickly, I wiped my eyes, turned and headed for home. When I arrived home, Mom met me and put her arm around my shoulder. "Gailen, you did the right thing. You did what you had to do." She did not punish me. With her firm voice of guidance, I learned that I had to correct the mistake I made by returning the truck I had taken.

I felt unsettled. Why did Mrs. Good speak so kindly to me? I had expected her to yell at me. I knew from the look on Mom's face, when she saw the truck in my pocket, that she was disappointed. Would she tell Dad? Would he punish me? Would Mom tell Joanna, Bill and Roland? Would they tease me?

I felt uncomfortable for several days. Nothing happened. To my knowledge, Mom did not tell anyone. As I write these words, I remember feeling sad for what I had done by taking Fred's truck and for disappointing Mom. I said to myself, "I will never do that again." Mom's treatment of me was effective.

My first year in college, I took a general psychology course. We discussed how difficult it was to change human behavior, especially the behavior of criminals. The next time I was alone with Mom, I asked her, "Do you remember the time I stole Fred's red truck and what you did to teach me right from wrong?"

Mom replied, "Yes, I do. Why do you ask?"
I looked into her eyes, "I want you to know that the way you treated me and what you taught me rehabilitated your "little thief."

"I knew you would learn from your experience." Mom stepped toward me and gave me a hug. She was breathing into my chest and whispered, "I love my ex 'little thief.' "

My eyes were moist. I pressed my face into her brown hair which was streaked with white and whispered, "I love you."

45

We walked to the door together. I picked up my book bag. As we walked on to the porch, I said, "Mom, I have accounting class this afternoon. I am doing fine."

"I wish you well in everything you do," she said. I walked down the steps and ran to my car. I opened the door and looked across the top of the car. This house was a different location than the back porch steps on Fern Street. However, Mom stood on the steps just like she did when I turned to look at her in the alley behind Fred's house. This time, her right hand touched her lips and she threw me a kiss. My heart raced with joy.

JOANNA'S SCHOOL ON THE STEPS

Joanna had just completed the fourth grade. She was enthused about what she had learned from her teacher, Miss Miller. Mom told Joanna, "Miss Miller is a very good teacher."

Joanna replied, "I know. I want to be a teacher like her." During the first week after school ended, Joanna went recruiting for students.

Roland and I were already in the class. We had no choice. However, I wanted Joanna's teaching to add to what she had already taught me about school. Roland had completed first grade. Joanna thought he needed additional help with his concentration and arithmetic.

She knew most of the young children and their mothers in our neighborhood. Her recruiting efforts resulted in five students –three girls and two boys. The mothers were happy to cooperate because this activity would keep their kids busy and reduce their boredom, as well as the mothers' stress.

In June 1935, Joanna created her school on the steps. At the first class, she said, "If someone is mean, they can take your doll or your scooter, and you may never see it again. But when you learn something and it is in your head, no one can take that from you."

Each Saturday at ten o'clock, the students gathered on the wide steps leading up to our front porch. Joanna stood behind a small desk that Dad bought at a neighborhood sale. The term garage sale had not yet been invented since some of the houses did not have garages.

Like a trained teacher, Joanna, at age ten, had her lesson plan – just like Miss Miller. The first event of the day was the pledge to the flag. This flag that Joanna made was unique. It was drawn with crayons on a sheet of cardboard. It had thirteen red and white stripes and the forty eight stars in the upper left corner. Hawaii and Alaska had not yet joined the Union.

The academics began with learning the alphabet. Joanna had us draw the letter "A" then pronounce it followed with saying a word that began with A. Each student did three letters at every class period. This was fun!

Arithmetic followed. The use of the term, math, didn't come into vogue for several years. Joanna used Popsicle sticks and round-headed clothespins for her teaching aids. She showed us five objects in her hand then put her hands behind her back. When she brought her hands to the front, and there were only three objects, she would ask, "How many did I 'take away?'" Instead of the word subtraction, she used the words "take away" which was easy for us five and six year olds to understand.

Next, Joanna told us a story. She chose one she had written or one from her school Reader. To test our memory and comprehension, she would ask questions. "Who was the main character? What was his or her first name? What was the story about? What did the main character do that was good?" The way Joanna taught was effective.

Play time came next. "All work and no play makes Jack a dull boy," she told us. Games of jump rope, hop scotch, hide-and-seek and catch and throw provided physical activity and increased our heart rate.

Each session ended with a treat. During the previous week, Joanna made extra cookies and cupcakes when Mom was baking. When she had not done so, cookies from the Kitchenette bakery filled the bill. It did not surprise me that most of the students showed up each week.

I entered first grade in the fall after eleven weeks of school on the steps. Mom told my teacher, Miss Anderson, about Joanna's school, so she did not call on me very often to answer questions. Because it was mostly repetition of what I already knew, the classroom work was easy for me. One girl came to me and said, "Gailen, you are really smart." My reply, "No, I am not smarter than you. I've had preschool education which gives me a head start."

Thank you, Joanna, my dear, for giving me a head start. Your teaching helped me to develop my confidence so that I was never afraid of going to a new school or entering a new class or taking exams. This confidence stayed with me all the years of my formal education – and is with me today – as I venture into my retirement years.

I still can remember hearing Joanna's young voice stating: "If someone is mean, they can take your doll or your scooter, and you may never see it again. But when you learn something and it is in your head, no one can take that from you."

COLD WINTER DAYS AND NIGHTS

The back bedroom of our Fern Street house was a painting surface for Jack Frost. All four of us children shared the room. In the cold winter with no central heating, the moisture from four sets of lungs over a night time created layers of ice upon the window. Sometimes, the ice did not completely melt during the day. Then at night, it froze again and another layer of ice was created. When I asked, "How does this happen?" Joanna, my eleven year old sister, with whom I shared the bed, replied, "Jack Frost put it there. It's one of his paintings."

I delighted in watching the shifting colors of refracted light as the rising sun shined through the branches of a tree outside. The shadow - cast by the branches - continued its broken pattern through the rippled colored ice on the window pane. What a wonderful sight - multicolored. After this view of beautiful art, I cuddled down into the bundle of cozy blankets for what Joanna called, "a few more winks."

Getting dressed on a cold Kansas morning, in a just above freezing house, was like the Olympics – full of fast and furious action. Before going to bed, the older four of us would place our clothes on the dining room table. In the morning when our warm feet hit the cold floor, we would rush into the dining room and quickly put on our socks. Then, off came the warm pajamas and on went the ice cold underwear and the clothing of the day. The heat from the gas Coleman stove felt so good. We would watch the dancing red hot flames of the stove through the small isinglass windows in rows across the bottom. Jay Roy was the only one who didn't experience this early ritual. At one year old - he could sleep as late as he wanted.

"Don't get too close or bump anyone," Mom admonished. No repeat warning was necessary. Learning comes quickly when you touch a hot Coleman stove, whether the touching is a finger, an elbow or part of your behind.

Looking through the doorway as I dressed, I saw Mom as she passed between the kitchen stove and the table. Preparing a hot breakfast of either oatmeal from the round box with the blue Quaker man on front or Cream of Wheat from its yellow box was her daily task.

On top of the Coleman stove in the dining room, sat a kettle of boiling water that Mom used to make us hot cocoa. The toast was made by pulling out a drawer at the bottom of the gas kitchen stove that held a metal rack. Mom laid the bread slices on the rack and the heat of the rack toasted the bread.

"Don't bother Mom," Joanna reminded us. "If we interrupt Mom while she's toasting, it might get really crisp."

Once the cups of hot cocoa were put on the table, I dunked my crispy toast whether it was brown or black. Nothing was wasted. It tasted good. Then, off to school.

YOU CAN'T HIDE FROM DAD

I practiced my act on the back porch until I had it almost perfect. I went to the living room to perform it for Jay Roy, my three-year-old brother. I took a full glass of water with me. The trick was: I would hold the glass in my left hand, open my right hand as wide as I could, then place the glass of water in the palm of my right hand. When I thought it was steady and I was ready, I would release my left hand, leaving the glass to balance on my right hand without using any fingers.

It worked on the back porch. It worked now - for a few seconds. The glass began to wobble. I grabbed for it with my left hand and caught it. The glass tipped and its water went on the floor. Correction - it landed in the middle of Mom's pretty oval rag rug - one of her prized possessions.

I panicked. All I could think of was, I had made a "big" mistake. For big mistakes Dad might apply his razor strap that hung on the back of the bathroom door.

I handed Jay Roy the empty glass and headed out the door. Quickly, I was off the porch and headed down the street - running. Half a block away, I hid behind the trunk of a big Elm tree. With my arms pressed down along my sides I could not be seen from our front porch. I found a perfect place to hide.

I peeked out just a little near a big break in the heavy bark that ringed the tree. I saw Dad out on the sidewalk looking in both directions, and shouting, "Gailen, Gailen." I did not answer. I saw him go up and down both sides of the house. I scrunched even tighter behind the tree. I looked again, he was gone.

After five or six minutes – which seemed like hours, I went back home. .Slowly I walked through the open front door. Dad came to me. He put his hand on my shoulder, and said, "I was so worried. I looked and looked – even went back to the alley and looked in the barn. I could not find you. Where were you?"

"Behind a big tree."

52

Mom came into the room with a bucket and a handful of rags. Dad took the bucket and handed the rags to me. On my hands and knees, I pressed the rags into the soggy rug. I handed Dad the rags. He took them and squeezed them over the bucket. Back to me they came – over and over again. When the water was wiped from the wooden floor and I thought none was left in the rug, Dad took the rags from me. He bent down on one knee and pressed the rags into the rug again. Like magic, more water appeared.

After a few more presses, squeezes and wringing out of the rags, he said, "There, I think that will do it."

Mom went outside and was sweeping the front porch. Dad called to her, "Leah, how are you doing?"

"The porch is ready," she replied. Dad picked up one end of the rug and motioned for me to pick up the other end. I gripped the rug and lifted with all my might. It was heavy. I used all of my seven year old strength to lift my end. Together, we put it on the porch - and spread it out to dry. Mom was standing on the ground beside the porch, making sure that the rug did not hang over the edge and touch the ground. "Stick close to home this afternoon," Dad said, looking at me. "We'll need to turn it over then."

Later that day, the rug was dry. Dad and I put it back in the living room. Mom commented, "It looks cleaner - the colors a little brighter." There had been no mention of the razor strap.

I learned two lessons from this event:
#1: You can't hide from Dad, because you always have to go home.
#2: If you make a mess, clean it up. You won't be punished.

My parents were effective teachers.

BREAKING BREAD TOGETHER

Every Friday afternoon, Dad came home later than usual. All of the shelves in the stores on his route were filled with Kitchenette bread for the following Saturday–the big shopping day of the week. Shopping on Sunday, except for medicine emergencies, was against the "Blue Laws" in Kansas.

Dad's coming home was an exciting event. He brought with him a large paper bag full of broken loaves of bread and a sack of broken oatmeal cookies. The salesmen at the bakery rotated weekly to receive these free delicious treats. In Dad's huge right hand was a gallon jug of milk with an inch of yellow cream across the top. Milk came in gallon glass bottles. He gave the jug a hearty shake and put it in the ice box.

After supper, we all pitched in to wash the dishes and put them away. When the task was done, we took our places around the large kitchen table. Mom gave each of us a bowl filled with cool milk. It had been sitting on the ice in the ice box.

When I received my bowl, I dipped several pieces of the broken bread and cookies into the cold milk. Then, into my mouth they went. As I pressed them together on my tongue, I thought, "What a sweet delicious treat." The bread turned sweet as it mixed with my saliva and the rich milk. An occasional bite of cookie was mixed in with the bread. This was a dessert I ranked above all others.

After all seven of us were served, Dad began the family conversation. "Each of you will have a turn to talk – one at a time with no interrupting."

Dad always went first. He told stories about traffic on the streets, crowded stores and the chatter at the Kitchenette Bakery. Mom shared from the conversations she had with neighbors, at PTA meetings, and told of the news on the radio. We kids told of happenings with our friends, events at school and personal projects we were working on. Each person spoke, as we proceeded around the table. All listened. No stage fright or nervousness was evident. We ate our sweet dessert, talked and laughed – and laughed some more. The Great Depression had not killed our spirits. I did not realize that we were poor.

I entered high school in 1945. All freshman students were required to take two semesters of speech class. Miss Perkins, my teacher, called it the "Elocution Class." Some of the students would literally freeze when they had to stand before the class and give a speech. I was relaxed and enjoyed the class. The family conversations over many years prepared me for my assignments. After I spoke, Miss Perkins said to me, "Well done."

Mom reminded me of past events that I included in some of my speeches. She commented, "If you are alert, you can learn something worthwhile every day. Later in your life, you may want to use this."

The teachers in my high school prepared grade cards for us to take home to our parents. Mom looked at mine and saw the "A" and the positive comments written by Miss Perkins. "Gailen, I am so pleased that you are doing well." Then, she hugged me around my shoulders.

I went outside to play. Sounding in my head were Mom's pleasant voice and words of approval. As I walked, then ran toward the junior high basketball court, I felt much taller than my 5' 10" physical height.

Mom graduated from Severy, Kansas, Rural High School. Her favorite class was Elocution. "In Elocution Classes, I learned to articulate my words and express myself in a bold, forthright way. Women of my age tended to be timid, to hold back what they were thinking. I am so glad I had those classes."

I was glad that she was my Mom.

FIRST SEX EDUCATION

Joanna, Bill and Roland were at school. I was playing in the yard. As I came around the corner of the porch, I saw in the shadows of the steps an unusual sight. Kitty appeared to be trying to get something out of her stomach. As I came closer, I saw several very small water soaked kittens lying on Kitty's stomach. Excited, I ran into the house - calling, "Mommy, Mommy come quick."

Mom came outside. We saw Kitty retreating under the porch to the far corner toward a pile of leaves blown in by the wind. Mom ran up the steps, into the kitchen, retrieved a flashlight and returned. She pointed it toward the place where Kitty lay. "There are 1, 2, 3, 4 little kittens" she said. Quickly she handed me the flashlight and raced up the steps.

I pointed the flashlight toward the leaves. Kitty raised her head up and down. She picked the kittens up one at a time and licked them. Each would let out a tiny cry as she placed it on her stomach. When all were on her stomach, there was silence. The kittens were nursing.

Mom returned with a saucer filled with milk. She placed it under the porch as far as she could reach. Beside the saucer, Mom placed a piece of toast and a strip of bacon. Standing up, she reached out her hand. Her fingers caressed my head and ruffled the blond hair on my head.

"I'll look in a little later and see how she's doing." She returned to the kitchen in silence. I turned my head for one more look, then stood up and went inside to put the flashlight in its special drawer. I felt happy. I had four new kittens and a Mom whose loving touch comforted me.

Mom was in the pantry moving things around. She was searching for something. Emerging from the pantry, she held a small wooden box in one hand and a piece of a blanket in the other. She put the blanket into the box and handed it to me. "Put this on the back

56

porch where Kitty usually has her food and water. I think she will bring her kittens to it." And Kitty did so the next day.

After several weeks of feeding and playing with the kittens, Mom announced, "As delightful as the kittens are, it is time for them to go."

"Please, can't we keep them?" was the universal cry.

"No. We need food for our own meals."

The news about the kittens spread fast. We had many requests for "mousers."

Only Mom and I knew what I had seen a few weeks before. I was curious about what had happened. There was no explanation coming forth. The questions I had in my mind reoccurred for several months and from time to time over the years. Adults did not share information with their children about sex or the birth process in those days.

SAYING GOODBYE TO KITTY

"Parting Is Such Sweet Sorrow"
– <u>Wm. Shakespeare</u>

We drove to our new home on South Water Street in Dad's bread truck. When we arrived in front of the house, Joanna, my twelve year old sister, picked Kitty up in her travel box. Kitty had been showing severe signs of aging for several months. She was less alert and no longer chased mice.

Mom instructed Joanna, "Hold Kitty in your arms and walk with her around the house. Do not put her down until she lets you know that she wants down. Becoming frightened would not be good for Kitty."

Joanna would be thirteen in June. She was two years old when she got Kitty as a kitten. That would make Kitty eleven years old. Eleven years seemed like a long time to me.

Joanna and I sat on the porch floor tearing newspapers into little pieces. These were to be used to line and soften a second sleeping and litter box for Kitty. She could now sleep in two places without having to move the box. We hoped that Kitty would not be tempted to go outside to relieve herself.

The back porch had one more step than the one at our old house. Kitty struggled going down them. Joanna would often carry her down the steps so she could walk around outside. Kitty went into the barn at the rear of our property only once that I know of. She wasn't looking for mice anymore.

Then it happened. The afternoon temperature was 98 degrees. Even so, Kitty was half- covered by her blanket as she slept. Roland was the first to notice. Her front legs were stretched and stiff. She was not sleeping. She was dead.

Mom gathered all five of us children together. "Kitty will no longer suffer. She has been a member of our family for eleven years - and deserves a proper funeral and burial. We need to do it before dark. Each of you, one by one, can kneel down right here and pet her fur." After each of us had done so, Joanna covered Kitty with the white handkerchief Mom handed her.

Dad returned from a trip to the filling station and received the sad news. "I need to leave soon and return to the bakery. We have to move some equipment."

Supper was eaten in silence. I observed that none of us seemed to be very hungry. Is anybody hungry before a funeral?

We washed and put away the dishes. Bill was out by the barn digging the grave. We decided, while still on the back porch, that Kitty would be buried in her sleeping box.

Dad called into the bakery. He told them that he wanted to be with his family and would not be able to help them.

Jay Roy stayed in the house with Dad. Joanna led the procession, carrying Kitty in her box. Bill leaned his shovel against the barn and joined us. We stood around the grave. Joanna gently laid the box in the hole. She stood up, folded her hands in front of her chest and said, "Please take good care of Kitty." Then she began crying - softly. Bill took out his handkerchief to blow his nose. Roland stood erect with his hands at his side, just like a soldier. A big tear drop filled each of my eyes.

Kneeling around the open hole, Mom tossed a handful of dirt onto the white handkerchief. The rest of us followed – handful after handful until the hole was filled. I was both glad and sad – glad that Kitty was no longer suffering, sad that I had lost a playmate. I remembered Fern Street and the moments playing with Kitty under the table on the cool linoleum floor on hot afternoons..

Just before bedtime, Roland was sitting near Joanna. He asked, "Do cats and kittens go to a special place like a kitty heaven?" Joanna replied, "I think they go to the same place people do. People would need cats and kittens in heaven."

This was my introduction to death – the finality of life. I realized that Kitty would no longer chase the yarn ball that I threw. She was gone for good. Only my memories of her remained – and the small wooden cross next to the barn.

I felt sad. I was not frightened. Somehow, I understood that this was the life cycle: a birth, a life lived, a death. I believe it helped me accept the death of my grandfather Keeling - the deaths of my parents, my sister and brothers – and eventually, even my own death.

First, the grieving process – then, the letting go – and finally, the getting on with life.

INTRODUCTION TO NEW WORLD[12]

By Gailen Keeling

At Riverside Park in Wichita, Kansas,
Our family had a picnic almost every Saturday evening.
The movie was projected onto a concrete wall
That rose 12 feet into the air.

As darkness began to fall in the western sky,
I took a front- row seat to see the opening comedy.
It was usually the hilarious Key Stone Cops.
This was followed by a Tom Mix cowboy movie.

Tom rode in on his white stallion, wearing his cowboy hat,
Firing his six-shooter, with an endless number of shots.
A hero he was when he drove the bad guys out of town.

The movies in the park were fun to watch
But they did not prepare this 9-year-old boy
For the wonderful *Wizard of Oz* (1939).
It was the first movie I saw in a real movie theater.

With the speakers blaring – the Munchkins sang
 "We're off to see the Wizard."
Dorothy skipped up the Yellow Brick Road
Toward the Castle of the Wizard of OZ.
I remember Dorothy saying, in a dramatic voice,
"Toto, this doesn't look like Kansas anymore."
And the Land of Oz certainly did not.

She held Toto in her arms.
Beside her walked
The barrel-chested friendly lion,
The dancing straw scarecrow,
And the squeaking tin man.

---

[12] Copyright©2014 Gailen Keeling

As Judy Garland's mellow voice captured me and
Took everyone in the theater along with her,
We joined the bluebirds flying "Over the Rainbow."

I remember Billie Burke, the friendly fairy,
Who rescued Dorothy from the Wicked Witch of the West,
Who had threatened Dorothy with, "I'll get you my Little Pretty."

The magical Wizard liked Dorothy and helped her return to Kansas.
She regained consciousness in the comforting arms of Auntie Em,
Who eased her fears as she wiped the blood from her brow
Where debris from the tornado had hit her and knocked her
unconscious.

From her exciting trip to Oz
Dorothy returned to a bright, new Kansas.

As I left the movie house,
So did I.

ON CHARACTER BUILDING

You cannot dream yourself into a character; you must hammer and forge yourself one.
Henry David Thoreau

Parents can only give good advice or put them on the right path, the the final forming of a person's character lies in their own hands.
Anne Frank

DAVID'S ILLNESS
AND MY TRIP TO SANTA BARBARA[13]

By Debbie Nichols Poulos

We settled into our new house at 4012 Bernice Drive in Point Loma in the summer of 1945. Daddy went off to work each day, driving about 20 miles inland to campus. There just wasn't a lot of housing yet out near San Diego State College where he was a chemistry professor. Being close to the ocean, however, in Point Loma was a most desirable location for Mom and us kids.

I know that we made frequent trips to the sands of La Jolla Shores, a beautiful straight stretch of white sandy beach where waves rolled in above the contours of the shallowly sloping ocean floor.

As I was an infant and toddler, I don't have much of a memory of the early outings to the beach. However, Mom would have packed sandwiches, fruit, and milk, or healthy snacks; spread out a blanket; propped up the umbrella; unfolded her beach chair; and pulled out buckets and shovels. She could relax, read, and visit with a friend, while she watched David, and as I grew older, me, as we contentedly played in the sand and waded into the shallow surf. It was very safe for Mom to watch us from a distance while we splashed and giggled. Those days at the beach must have been idyllic.

The idyll ended soon after one of these days at the beach in late September 1947, when I was two and a half and David was four and a half. It would be the events of this day and the weeks that followed that would create my first vivid memory as a child.

Evidently, we had stayed in the water after it started to cool down and David had gotten chilled. Later it was speculated that the fruit he'd eaten earlier in the day at a friend's house hadn't been washed. At any rate, David came down with a fever.

Our family doctor couldn't give a specific diagnosis, but with his flu-like symptoms David was in bed for a couple of weeks. He had begun to experience difficulty walking. Finally, when his recovery didn't come and the effects of his symptoms worsened, he was given an earth-shattering diagnosis— POLIO.

He was hospitalized, in quarantine, where batteries of tests were run. There is an entire back story to all of this that I will detail at some point to explain, perhaps, why our family has a vulnerability to viruses and neuromuscular illnesses, but that must wait for another day.

The two-week delay in a specific diagnosis meant that David had not been immobilized in order to minimize the virus's invasion of his muscle tissue, as he would have been if polio had been suspected. With the unrestricted activity of a four year old, even a sick and lethargic four year old, David's leg muscles had sustained irreparable damage. During the next twelve months, David received acute hospital care, followed by a convalescent hospital where he received daily physical therapy. This included aqua therapy where his atrophied leg muscles were exercised, massaged, and encouraged in every way known to modern medicine.

When the physical therapy regime proved disappointing, he returned to the hospital for surgery, which removed healthy muscle tissue from his abdomen and grafted it into his legs. The outward results of these surgeries were evidenced by railroad-track scars that ran up and down his legs and across his belly. The surgeries, like the therapies before them, proved futile in restoring muscular competence to David's legs. Finally, a regimen of physical therapy that taught David how to walk with braces that stiffened his legs and crutches with which he could propel himself, using the healthy muscles of his upper body, proved a success.

I don't remember much of what David went through during this period. I just learned these details many years later as I questioned my parents about what had happened. All I knew was what happened to me around this time. It is the earliest recollection of my childhood, as it was traumatically and indelibly imprinted on my memory. I was two and a half.

It must have been at the height of the crisis that my parents decided to take me to my grandparents in Santa Barbara. These were my mom's parents, Walter and Ruth Seward. I knew them well as they came to San Diego and we drove to Santa Barbara for frequent visits. They lived in the top floor of a big two-story Victorian home on Chapalla Street, just one street off State Street near the heart of downtown Santa Barbara. They were caretakers of the property and of the elderly woman who owned it.

My dad and I headed off on the train; I believe it was the Pacific Coast Daylight that traveled along the land's edge making its way up the coast. It started as a delightful trip for me, just Daddy and me, alone together on an adventure, a rare treat for me. He held me on his lap, pointing out the scenery as we went. I sometimes stood on his lap for a better view of the ocean or other sights as we made our way north.

Upon our arrival at the station in Santa Barbara, Ruth and Walter, my grandparents, were there to greet us. Suddenly, however, my dad handed me over to my grandparents and rushed off to make the next train back to San Diego. I screamed bloody murder, but with no success in changing the plan as it unfolded. I screamed, squirmed, and fought to get out of my grandfather's arms and run to my father. But there was no getting away. I cried and cried at being suddenly abandoned by my father. It didn't matter that I was with my loving grandparents.

This is my second earliest clear and persistent memory. I don't believe my father had prepared me for what was going to happen. I suppose he might have believed that an almost two and a half year old would not have comprehended such information. So in the absence of that, I believed that both my father and I were going up to Santa Barbara for a visit, not that I was going to be left there by myself.

It doesn't matter now, but I do believe that children that young can understand such information. In the absence of this preparation, I was completely traumatized by what happened. This was my parental abandonment incident. I could not change or control what happened. All I could do was adjust and deal with it. I don't know how a two and a half year old does this, but that is what I did. In a way, I think I figured that from now on the only person I could count on was myself.

In photographs from this period I look very serious. I'm at the beach with grandma and grandpa, or playing with a puzzle on the second floor front balcony. I had adjusted to my new life with my grandparents. They were loving and attentive. We played together, went on walks to the beach, worked on baking projects in the kitchen, visited with grandma's friends, went to the Christian Science Church Grandma attended. They clearly loved having me with them.

Grandma even took me to sit for a pastel drawing and oil painting by a local artist, Marjorie C. Murphy. We went regularly for several days for these sittings, supposedly planned around my nap time. I remember sitting in a highchair with little toys to play with while Marjorie talked to me and painted. My grandma sat nearby.

Photo by Dan Brown

Then one day my mom and dad showed up at my grandparent's house. I was happy to see them, but I did not expect what happened next. They packed me up, put me in the car, and we headed back to San Diego. I cried bloody murder again. I had come to be comfortable with Grandma and Grandpa and had come to expect that this was where I would remain. I believe I'd been there for six weeks. For a child my age it must have seemed like forever.

I believe this trauma was temporary, but it did lead me to believe that I couldn't anticipate what might happen to me. I know a child of my age would not have conceptualized trust issues. But over the years as I replayed these events, I came to believe that my parents weren't entirely trustworthy. This early abandonment was the first traumatic event of my young life. It would be remembered and interpreted for years to come.

Note: *The Marjorie C. Murphy oil portrait was featured in a show shortly after it was finished. I have the 1948 newspaper article that describes it. Eventually Grandma acquired the pastel and the oil painting. After grandma died my mom received them. Mom gave the pastel to me at that time. When mom died I inherited the oil.*

David and Debbie with 9 mo. old baby sister Eleanor

Debbie and David

FROM FAILURE TO SUCCESS[14]

By Deborah Nichols Poulos

I've told this story many times over the last several years, and I've been urged to share it more widely. Recently, I decided that its time had come. It's about my difficulties, failure, as an elementary school student learning to read. And, ultimately, it is about my success. I believe it is a cautionary tale.

In 1950 when I entered kindergarten, five year olds were not taught to read. Kindergarten was a year to learn socialization skills and to engage in imaginary play. It wasn't until first grade that reading instruction began. But even then there was no single approach. Some schools postponed actual reading instruction in favor of "reading readiness" activities. Students learned to recognize letters of the alphabet and engaged in other non-reading activities. When reading instruction began some teachers used a "phonetic" approach, while others relied on learning a "sight" vocabulary, later known as the "whole language" approach.

When I started first grade I was in San Diego at Andrew Jackson Elementary School, not far from San Diego State, where my dad was a chemistry professor. We were still working on "reading readiness" activities when, in October, our family made the move to Oak Ridge, Tennessee, where my dad would work at the National Radiation Lab.

I was very familiar with books. My parents had read to me often. I enjoyed listening to the stories and loved to examine the illustrations, picking out details in the pictures that were referred to in the words read by my mom or dad. After the reading, usually at bedtime, I'd

---

73

"reread" the stories by myself, turning the pages and looking at the pictures for the clues I needed to retell the stories, sometimes over and over again. But never had I linked the words I heard telling the stories with the words printed on the pages. I don't know that I even thought of the printed words as the source of the stories.

I was, however, acutely aware that first day at Woodland School that I was the stranger. Everyone else had been together since the beginning of the school year. I was new, different, arriving late, coming all the way from San Diego, California. I didn't look any different from the other kids, but I sure sounded different. I remember feeling an intense sense of being studied by everyone, both children and adults, in this new classroom. And as I sat with the others, waiting for my turn to "read," I knew that I was going to be revealing something to everyone about who I was. And then it happened, "Debbie," I heard the teacher say my name, "It's your turn." I had been concentrating so hard on listening to the other children read, that I had not noticed that the child just to my right had finished her turn.

I took a breath and began to attack my sentence, one word at a time. Of course, I don't remember the sentence, but I do remember the excruciating anguish, frustration, embarrassment, and humiliation I felt as I struggled along from word to word, sometimes guessing right, sometimes guessing wrong, and sometimes having no idea what to say. The teacher corrected me or filled in the correct next word, and the next word, until I had made it to the period at the end. I knew this little dot marked the end of my turn.

There were two more readers after me, but I no longer paid any attention. I didn't look at the book and I didn't listen to the words. All of my attention was inside my own head, my own body. I think the sound inside my head was like that of ocean waves crashing on a sandy beach, and the scene before my eyes was like the snow or diagonal lines on a television screen. My distraction was soon interrupted by the voice of the teacher and the movement of the children seated around me. It was time for our little group to get up and return to our desks, while another group of kids positioned themselves in a line in front of the book.

I watched from my desk as student after student took his or her turn to read a sentence from the book. It was clear to me that I was the only one in the class who had had so much trouble completing the sentence correctly. I was in pain, and I didn't know what to do about it. I felt helpless, sad, and alone. I can't know whether I hid my feelings or not, but I didn't tell anyone what had happened or how I felt. Even when I went home, if I shared what had happened, it didn't register in any way that this was a problem that needed to be addressed by adults. The problem, if there was one, was mine. I knew there was a problem and I knew it was me.

The scenario of the first day was to repeat itself over and over again. The second day I was called to read, on the "firing line," with a different group. At first I worked and worked trying to find the key to unlock the mystery. I paid close attention as my classmates read, I looked at the illustrations in the book, and I began to identify many words I could remember and read.

Yes, I had picked up the big content words; the "picture words" like wagon, house, the dog Spot; the name words like Dick and Jane, and the color words like white and red. I could associate these words with the pictures, the words that had meaning to me. All the other words made no vivid connection. Words like "were, went, with, want, work, when, where, and them, these, those, this, they, than, then," were a complete mystery to me. No matter how closely I paid attention, no matter how hard I tried, I could never remember which word was which. How was I to know one from the other? They were all just a mess of letters that looked too much the same to me. I had no way to figure out which word to say out loud when I saw words like these in one of "my" sentences.

These were the words, years later as a teacher, I would call the "glue words." Without these words the sentences would not hold together. Try as I might the sentences I was asked to read always fell apart. Teachers and other students tried to help me as I stumbled

75

during my turn to read out loud in the group. But their efforts only lasted as long as it took for me to get to the end of the sentence. Each time I was presented with these mysterious "glue words," and many other words, I failed. I couldn't remember all the new words.

I remember what I'd call "reading lessons." We'd sit on the floor in front of an easel on which the teacher had written a couple of columns of words. The little group would read the words along with the teacher, and the teacher talked about the words. Sometimes the words rhymed. Sometimes the words began with the same letter, or were spelled the same in different parts, or had some other common element, such as all appearing in the same story.

Even though I could follow along with the group and repeat the words as the teacher recited them, I didn't come away from those little group lessons with any sense of how to unlock the mystery of the words when I was alone. When I came upon those words again, on my own or when I was asked to read in front of the group, I just couldn't remember which word to say that was a match for the word or words on the page.

No one had bothered to find out what preparation I'd had for being asked to read. As a child I figured that if an adult asked me to do something, I was supposed to know how to do it. This was my first experience with failure, and it was excruciating. I understood immediately that all of these first potential friends now knew I was stupid. There was no other explanation to my six-year-old mind. They were expected to read, and they did. I was expected to read, but I didn't.

I'm sure I tried very hard at first. But before long I must have decided to quit. Whenever I had to read in front of the group my failures were all too obvious to me and everyone else. Whenever I was supposed to be reading alone at my seat, my only comfort was in knowing that no one but I knew that I couldn't make sense of the words on the page, didn't know the story as it was written, and couldn't, as I was asked to do so many times, "go back to my desk and read the story silently to myself." I couldn't answer questions about the story, unless the answers were revealed through the illustrations, as fortunately, at least in the simpler, early stories, they often were. At first, I got enjoyment out of "reading" the pictures for meaning and at least telling myself the "picture story." But the pleasure in this diversion soon disappeared.

Although all of my senses were on high alert during my reading circle's oral reading sessions, when I returned to my desk my strategy was avoidance. When I was sent back to my seat "to read the story silently to myself," instead of reading, I looked out the classroom windows, watched the clouds move, listened to the birds, daydreamed about what I would do when the reading period ended or when we would go outside to play. I knew I had to hold the book as if I were reading it, as I had been told to finish reading the story silently at my desk. I became good at sitting at my desk, looking at the pages, turning the pages, but I no longer really saw what was printed there. Finally, I closed the book as if I were doing what I'd been told to do and set it down. Now I could go on to something that I enjoyed doing, something that I was good at.

The pain and humiliation of my reading failure was so intense, I had no incentive to continue to try to read when I had the respite of time on my own. My survival skill, when not in the reading group, was to do anything other than try to read.

These experiences continued throughout the rest of first grade, when I returned to San Diego for second grade, and on into third grade. If I was lucky and I guessed right in my group I might be bumped to a higher group. But no sooner would that happen than I would guess wrong and be dropped back down to the low group.

Call it the "red group" or the "bluebird group," we all knew we were in the dumb group. We all knew we were dumb. Of course, we were in school to learn, and I'm sure there were a lot of things that we learned. For me, reading was not one of them. Now our reading lessons took place while we sat in chairs that we carried into a circle with the teachers. We each had our own copy of a reading textbook, which we brought to the reading circle each day.

As I recall, there were three groups, each named for a color or a type of bird. The teacher decided on the name of the group and from time to time she moved a student from one group to another. But, as early fall faded into Halloween, Thanksgiving, and then Christmas, the groups became static and everyone knew his or her assignment for the rest of the year.

I remember that I was one of the students who bumped around from group to group early in the year, but by the time the leaves turned yellow and fell, I had taken my place as a regular member of what, regardless of the official group name meant to disguise its rank, I knew was the low group.

Evidently it hadn't been easy for Miss Bain, my second grade teacher, to determine where I belonged. Each time I joined a group and received a reading assignment my anxiety was intense, but not so intense as when I knew I would be called upon to read out loud in front of the group. And this, unfortunately, was destined to happen at least once almost every day.

It didn't take me long to realize that Miss Bain usually proceeded around the group in order from the child seated at her left. But at least often enough to keep us a little off balance she would begin in the opposite direction. And then there were those times that put me into high panic when she would skip around the group calling on each of us at random and asking us to read aloud. Although I knew I could do nothing to prepare for this last eventuality, my usual strategy was to sit somewhere in the middle of the circle, usually a child or two closer to Miss Bain's right side than her left.

My seating strategy was the only one I put into practice as I joined the reading group, for I had no strategy for the task of reading itself. For reading, the operable system was luck or chance. On any given day, for any given story, of for any given reading group the scenario was essentially the same. I'd use the time before I'd have to read aloud to listen intently to my group mates, and to look intently at the words and pictures printed on the page in front of me. As students closer and closer to me took their turns to read, I even gauged which sentence or sentences would be mine.

It was always difficult to strike a balance between using the reading knowledge of the kids who read before me to teach me the words I didn't know, or to try to jump ahead to find and practice the words in the sentences that would be mine to read. But regardless of how I calculated this equation, I usually failed to garner enough information to succeed with even one sentence, let alone to succeed with two or more.

I might get off the first word or two with a speed and confidence that belied by knowledge of the certain doom that would follow when I'd stumble, be interrupted with corrections, wait eagerly for someone to supply the word I didn't know, or simply give up in total frustration and shame, as my turn, my sentence or sentences were picked up and read by the next kid in my group. Even though I knew I had been revealed, once again, as the poor reader, reading failure that I was, at least I had survived yet another turn in the reading group, and with any luck at all the group's time with the teacher would run out before that indignity would pass to me again. And tomorrow would be another day.

I am aware that it was sometime during my second grade year that my reading failure had become complex. I mean, I knew I couldn't read, I had little hope of ever learning to read, and I knew that all of my peers and my teacher knew this too. I accepted this ignominious fate as a fact of life. I had no clue of any other approach than this. Had I seen any way out of this terribly painful reality I certainly would have jumped at it. But the fact is, I saw no way out. The tenacity that was second nature when it came to physical tasks was nowhere to be found when it came to reading.

I'm sure there were other kids in my class who had trouble reading too. After all I was always in a group with other kids who presumably, read, or more accurately didn't read, like me. But I was certainly too occupied with my own troubles to give much thought to others. In any case, there was no particular approach that I was aware of that was designed to help me, or the others, over this hurdle.

The reading portion of our school day followed essentially the same script day in and day out. We had a story assignment out of our reading text book, we were introduced to a selected list of vocabulary words that we would encounter in that day's story, we were expected to read the story silently to ourselves at our seats, and respond to certain workbook or worksheet exercises. Sometime during this "reading period" we would be called into the reading circle to discuss the story, but mostly to take turns reading aloud while everyone else in the group listened. Our turn in the group finished, we would return to our desks to complete the rest of the assignment tasks.

There was nothing in this routine that provided me with any help in figuring out words I didn't know, either in the special vocabulary list or in the textbook story, or, for that matter, in the workbook or worksheet pages. There were words that I learned, and I was aware that my bank of known words was growing, but these known words were only of help to me if they were the words I had to read. I memorized the words I knew. But I didn't know how to figure out other words I hadn't memorized. Unfortunately, there were many more words that I had not yet learned, and this number of unknown new words was growing all the time. I had no idea how to figure out words for myself.

So, life went on. There were other things to do in school besides reading, and I enjoyed them all. My favorite times at school were on the playground; that meant recess, lunchtime, or P.E. I excelled at all of these. And, I'm sure that to some extent because of my obvious reading deficiency, I tried harder in the areas of school life that did not depend upon reading ability. But even inside the classroom everything didn't revolve around reading. We participated in art activities and music. I was actively involved in all the activities of the school day.

By fourth grade my reading failure wasn't so painful. Rarely were we asked to read out loud unless we volunteered. When the teacher chose kids to read aloud he chose the good readers. So I began to relax and not worry so much about my failure. As long as it wasn't on public display it wasn't so much of a problem. It became easier for me to hide in plain sight.

I was with the same kids from third through sixth grades, so my classmates already knew I was one of the dummies. No amount of effort was going to change that. My avoidance survival strategy worked and so I continued to use it.

Of course over the years my skills and vocabulary grew, but unless I was required to read aloud I didn't choose to read. I may have given it a haphazard effort from time to time, but I never "read for pleasure." Why would I voluntarily subject myself to the emotional pain of confronting my failure? As long as I didn't try to read, I didn't have to face the humiliation. Avoidance worked. My survival strategy was intact.

I suppose to be fair to my teachers and parents, I did well enough in school that they didn't see my difficulties as the handicap, both educationally and emotionally, that I knew they were. After all, my motivation was to hide my failure as much as I could. Those were the days of E, S, N grading. "Excellent," "Satisfactory," or "Needs Improvement." I got mostly Ss and a few Ns. The common refrain on my report cards was that my "effort" was lacking. Well, that was certainly true. But it was equally true that no one had ever tried to teach me the key to unlocking words I didn't already know.

I'd heard the refrain "sound it out" till I thought I would scream. But these words meant nothing to me. No one had ever demonstrated what it meant. Or at least I couldn't figure it out reliably. And I certainly wasn't putting in the effort to try to figure it out on my own.

I was able to contribute to class discussions because I was a good listener. I was okay in math as long as I had help reading word problems. I was great at any activities requiring visual/spatial aptitude. I was good at sports. I was good at making friends. On the playground it didn't matter who could or couldn't read. I was a happy kid. And the trauma of having to read aloud in front of my classmates had long since passed, or so I thought...

It never occurred to me that my avoidance would not be a successful long-term strategy. All I was concerned about was the present, the short-term; the future didn't enter my mind. But when I entered seventh grade the tables were suddenly turned. Within the first week or so of my English class the teacher brought in a class set of Time magazines and announced that we were going to learn to read for understanding in this periodical. He said we'd start with the student closest to the door and continue until everyone had had a chance to read.

I had chosen the desk closest to the windows in the back of the room. I figured this was the best place to hide. Now I realized I was about to be found out. And these were not all the students with whom I'd been through elementary school who already knew of my reading failure. These were kids from about eight different elementary schools. Only three or four out of a class of thirty-five knew me. So my anticipation of hiding my failures from all these potential new friends was suddenly at risk. My avoidance survival strategy was suddenly turned on its head.

My attention became riveted on the text of the magazine as I listened to my classmates begin to read. Paragraph by paragraph my fellow students read down the columns of text, progressing down the columns of desks, toward me. There would be no hiding for me today.

I listened intently; matching the words on the page with what I heard my classmates read. My attention had never before been so tightly focused. I was riveted to the task. As my turn to read drew closer, I skipped ahead to anticipate which paragraph would be mine. I'd scan that paragraph for the same words a classmate had already read. If there were new words I worked and worked to figure them out. I listened to the content of the article to help me with appropriate words to fit the context.

I hoped that the class period would end before my turn came, but as the reading moved into my column of desks I knew I would not escape. I had to skip down to different paragraphs a few times, but I was gaining confidence. Finally, it was clear exactly which paragraph I would have to read. Thankfully it was a short one. I had a chance to work on it several times, reading it through again and again. I had figured out, or associated from what I had heard, all the words. Now all I had to do was read them calmly and fluidly as if it was no big deal.

As the student in the desk in front of mine finished reading, I took a deep breath and began to read. I read slowly but deliberately. I tried to remain calm. I reached the end of the paragraph without stumbling or missing a single word. I slumped in my seat as I breathed a huge sigh of relief. I was amazed with myself. I had actually fooled my teacher and all the students in my class into believing I knew how to read.

But the biggest feat, by far, was that I had fooled myself. This experience forced me to reevaluate my strategy. If I could succeed in reading a paragraph in Time magazine in just one class period, just think of what I could do if I worked on reading in my own time.

This experience flipped a switch, and I was suddenly motivated to work on reading. I focused my attention as never before on school assignments that required reading. I don't recall how long it took, but it wasn't long before I was reading everything I was required to read. I finally understood what "sound it out" meant, and I figured out how to use "context clues." I still did not read anything that wasn't required, but I did put a great deal of effort in on all my assigned work.

It seemed like almost overnight I was becoming a good student. My writing improved, my spelling improved, and my reading just seemed to take off. By eighth grade I had become a better than average student. By ninth grade I was getting mostly A's. By tenth grade, as a student in the "academic track," I was one of only two students in a class of over 700 to get straight A's.

My high school principal sent a letter to my parents congratulating them on my achievement. When I saw the letter I was outraged. My parents had had nothing to do with my achievement. Why wasn't I being congratulated? But my outrage didn't dim my satisfaction. I understood the irony of the situation. It wasn't until years later, however, that an even greater irony came to my attention.

It may have been during college, or maybe even after college, that I learned from my mother that I had been tested as "gifted." It had happened when I was five years old. One of my dad's colleagues at San Diego State, in the education department, wanted guinea pigs for giving intelligence tests. My parents gave permission, and Dr. Bjorn Karlsen tested me.

I can vaguely remember the experience as being like a game. He asked me questions, asked me to copy shapes and designs with paper and pencil, and asked me to identify different arrangements of shaded shapes. I had no idea the purpose of these activities, of course. Afterwards my parents were told that I had tested in the "gifted" range. I don't know whether they were given a specific IQ score. And that was that.

I seriously doubt whether knowing I was "gifted" would have made any difference in my experiences as a young student. It was clear, however, that my parents were not particularly concerned about my school performance. They believed it was, indeed, a matter of effort not aptitude, and my achievement, or lack thereof, was entirely up to me. They apparently believed that eventually I would do well. Obviously, I had kept my difficulties well hidden from them. I can't explain why they weren't more involved, however. It is a mystery to me.

My mother had been an English major in college and she had taught fourth grade for two years before getting married. She certainly could have or should have taken a more active role in determining what was going on with me and remediating it. On the other hand, things turned out fine in the end. These early experiences with failure turned me into a better teacher. I believed I had to try harder than others to succeed, and I did try harder. I developed a persistence to overcome obstacles in my path.

It is interesting to note that as a high school student I was only asked to write two book reports. I chose the books from my parents' bookshelves. They were *Kon-Tiki* by Thor Heyerdahl and *We* by Charles Lindberg. I didn't read either book. I read the fly leafs on the books' covers and found selected passages within the books. From this information I constructed my book reports. Years later I realized that I had chosen books that illustrated the classic struggle of man against nature. Perhaps these adventures resonated with my own individual struggle to survive despite what for me seemed like insurmountable odds.

I went on to college at UC Davis. At first I thought I would be a home economics major focusing on clothing design. I had been designing and sewing my own wardrobe since I'd taken a Singer sewing course the summer after seventh grade. But when I learned the home economics department was in the Ag School and that I would have to take a bunch of science classes I quickly changed my mind. I neither enjoyed nor was I particularly interested in science.

Next I decided I'd be a P.E. major. I was good at sports, and as a career path I could see being a P.E. teacher. But P.E. too required a number of basic science classes. I took physiological psychology and some other classes, but I was not looking forward to kinesiology. So, although I ended up with a P.E. minor, I dropped it as a major.

I finally settled on an English major. Given my lack of a reading background this was an odd choice. Most other English majors had grown up as avid readers. They'd read Nancy Drew and a whole range of other children's, young adult, and adult literature. I'd read none of that. I had no reading background at all. I'd faked the only two book reports I'd ever had to write.

As an English major each poem, essay, or novel I was assigned to read was entirely new to me. Each author was new to me. I was diligent in my studies, but I was certainly a far cry from the backgrounds of my classmates. I did well enough, but I did not distinguish myself as an English major.

It would have made a lot more sense for me to be a math major. But like so many girls of my era I had a fear of competing in math when I believed the boys were so much better at it than I was. I believed this despite the fact that I had really enjoyed and excelled at geometry and algebra in high school. I'd completed advanced algebra and trigonometry as a junior, but had stopped short of taking calculus. I'd been intimidated by the stories I'd heard about how difficult calculus was supposed to be. I eventually took calculus in grad school and found it easy.

I got my elementary teaching credential and taught for twenty-seven years, first through sixth grades. I was acutely sensitive to the needs of students who had difficulty reading. I intervened with them one on one so they didn't have to suffer in front of their peers. I did not make assumptions about their potential abilities based on their troubles reading.

Photo by Dan Brown

As a teacher I made a point of really getting to know each child. I found that the more I was able to relate one on one and understand each child, the more effective I was in teaching him or her. This was not just true with kids who struggled, but with all kids. I was able to identify kids whose abilities were "off the charts," and I could tailor activities to meet their unique needs.

Students of very high abilities, "gifted" students, needed reading and writing activities that addressed their unique needs. They needed spelling words that stretched their vocabularies. They needed math activities that focused more on concepts and patterns than on algorithms. In fact, all kids did better in math if it was taught in a conceptual, visual/spatial, hands-on manner.

So, perhaps, in the long run my struggles with learning to read served me well. These early difficulties certainly resulted in my developing a tenacity and a determination that ended up being integral parts of my personality. In retrospect I'm glad for my early challenges. At any rate, that's what happened and I certainly couldn't have a "redo" on any of it. So best to accept it and move on.

BUILDING CHARACTER[15]

By Deborah Nichols Poulos

In the Classroom: An Embarrassing Incident

As a second grader I was very compliant and well behaved. That was the least I could do to try to achieve a reputation as someone other than "reading failure." I really liked my teacher, Miss Bain. I remember that we sang a lot in her classroom. She would have us stand next to our desks, face her, and sing with great volume and enthusiasm. We prepared in this manner for several programs in which each classroom performed in front of the rest of the school.

I remember getting dressed up in a fresh white blouse and plaid skirt, dark shoes and white ankle socks for these performances. I stood up straight among my classmates, looking out at the audience, while I sang the words and melodies, as Miss Bain directed us with arms waving, her lips distinctly mouthing the words of the songs.

Miss Bain's classroom was well organized and her discipline was firm, yet warm. I clearly remember only one of Miss Bain's rules. We were not allowed to use the restrooms during class time, but only during our recesses. I don't know how Miss Bain intended this rule to work, but I understood it as an absolute prohibition.

I believe that, in part, due to my embarrassment over my reading difficulties, I made every effort to be well behaved. If I could not garner my teacher's favor with my reading skills, then I would apply extra effort in areas in which I could perform well. Following the teacher's rules was one such focus of my attention. The extreme to which I carried this determination illustrates something important, I think, about the development of my seven-year-old character. The incident is as vivid sixty years later as it was on that day.

Sitting at my desk, I realized that I needed to go to the bathroom. I looked at the clock and thought that I could wait until recess. Being a child who lived for time on the playground, it is not hard for me to imagine that I must have been too preoccupied with play to use any of my precious recess time to use the restroom. Whether this was the situation in this particular instance, I can't recall. I do, however, remember that my urgency increased, and I finally summoned enough courage to get up from my desk and walk across the room to where Miss Bain sat working with a small group of students seated on the floor in front of her. Unfortunately, however, I had waited too long. As I stood in front of Miss Bain I had already started to cry, so distressed was I about having to ask her for permission to leave class to use the restroom. But before Miss Bain could even answer, it was too late. The urine was running down my legs, wetting my socks and shoes as it grew into a puddle on the floor under me. I was mortified.

Some of what happened after that is a blur. My mother must have been called. She would have had to bring dry clothes for me to change into and clean me up. And I would have had to return to class repaired, at least on the outside. Beneath the dry clothes, shoes and socks I must have hidden a deep sense of dread about what my teacher and my classmates thought of me. Failure to read was one thing, but a seven-year-old's failure to control her bladder in public reached an entirely different level. I felt unimaginably humiliated and was sure that my classmates judged me to be one of the lowest of the low.

If this is what they thought of me, however, I couldn't let them know. I would have had to return to class with a brave face and carry on as if nothing unusual had happened. I did not withdraw from my classmates. Instead I pushed myself forward, forcing myself to be outgoing and social, and playing all that much harder on the playground.

On the Playground: The Rules of the Game

Although compliance was my chosen behavior in the classroom in front of my teacher, it was not a controlling factor in my behavior on the playground in interactions with my peers. In retrospect I see this, and other behaviors I describe here, as indicative of my emerging sense of self. While children are not little adults, they are little people. It is through circumstances just like the ones I describe that they begin to develop life strategies. My playground strategy contrasted with my classroom strategy.

Being quite self-conscious about my reading difficulties, in the classroom I usually preferred to fade into the background. On the playground, however, I was a different child. Rather than being compliant with respect to my peers, I was quick to stand up for myself. Playground games provided fertile ground for controversies among classmates.

Foursquare, for example, a common playground game, was rife with possibilities for differences of opinion. The players, both those in the four squares, as well as those in line awaiting their turns, determined who stayed in and advanced, and who was called out and had to return to the end of the line to await another turn.

Rulings in these playground games were not simply based on the players' honest assessments of the games' events, but were also based on politics. Politics for second graders meant who was liked, who was popular, who was friends with whom, who had good or poor skills at the game, and to some extent, who would or would not stand up for herself to dispute a call made by the others. One or more of these factors could, in any given game, determine how plays were called by the other children engaged in that particular game.

Therefore, it was sometimes necessary for an individual player, me in this instance, to assert that the ball had in fact landed inside the square, or outside the square, or that it had landed on the line. A "liner" meant the play had to be done over. Whether a ball was clearly inside or outside a particular square determined who would be called out and who would get to remain in and advance a square. The goal, always, was to advance from the first square to the fourth square, where one gained the honor and the power of being "server."

In the classroom I felt diminished. As a child on the playground I was not going to be put down. I worked hard to develop my playground skills, and once I was able to compete for the prize of the "server" position in foursquare, I was not going to be bumped out by a call against me that I judged to be unfair. Even a skinny little seven-year-old girl had to determine when to protest and when to accept the call that sent her to the end of the line.

What I thought my peers thought of me definitely entered into my decisions on the playground. My reading failure was becoming a more and more important determining factor in the development of my behavior, both in and outside the classroom. And my behavior, and what I learned from assessing the results it received, was determining my character.

As I look back I can see that these early lessons served me well in later life. They strengthened me in many ways. They helped instill in me tenacity and determination. In many ways, I considered myself an "underdog," and these early experiences helped me to persevere on behalf of others, as well as myself.

WORLD WAR II MEMORIES[16]
By Nancy Maynard

With the radio going, my mother and father in the front seat and Richard and me in the back, we slowly made our way down the lovely one-lane road that wandered through the water company property— down the hill covered with dry grass and an occasional live oak tree, across the dam and into a thick woods of madrone, live oak and cedar. At this point the road seemed very mysterious to me, because it was dark with just a little dapple of sun coming through. I knew that when we started up the hill again, we would come to the spring. With my nose pressed against the back seat window, I watched carefully for it and suddenly there it was. By this time Richard had had enough of this sitting in the car and began to fuss. My father stopped the car.

We were driving along Sawyer Camp Road on a "Sunday drive." My father hated these drives because he drove all over California during the week and the last thing he wanted to do was go for a drive on Sunday. Mother, on the other hand, cooped up with young children all week, just wanted to get out. With no money for entertainment, going for a drive was a cheap way to get a change of scenery, also a time for the whole family to be together.

About a mile down Sawyer Camp Road from where it left Skyline Blvd. (now Interstate 280), a natural spring spurted out of the bank along the road. Our ritual was to stop there and drink from the spring. Dad promised us that we could do that again and I looked forward to it. Dad drove a California state-owned car for his job as a vector control specialist. He was to use it only on the job, but our old Willys didn't have a radio and the state car did. That afternoon he took the state car to break up his boredom of driving by listening to the radio.

We all piled out. Richard and I ran across the road to the spring, located a couple of feet off the road. The stream of water was contained by a pipe protruding out of the bank about four feet up from the ground—just high enough that I could stand under it, turn my face up and catch the water in my mouth as it splashed down to hit the stones below. The ice cold water seemed sweet to me. We loved drinking without a cup and getting all wet, even though Mother reminded us several times to stay dry. After we had all had a long drink, we climbed back into the car and my father turned on the radio. No more music, just a serious sounding voice. My father and mother suddenly stopped their talking. They hushed Richard and me. A deep voice on the radio said, "At 7:50 this morning, the Japanese bombed Pearl Harbor."

Thus began my memories of World War II. For the next four years I felt that the war would never end. It seemed that it had been going on all of my life. When the answer to every question I asked was "Because of the war", I always asked, "Will it ever be over?" I was assured that it would.

Even though we lived close to the coast of California with frequent air raid drills, my family managed to keep this from being a fearful time. Air raid drills were fun. If we were at school, we were all shepherded out of the classroom and into the hall, where we sat against the wall–away from the windows–with our heads between our knees. This was a fun break in the day. We all took it very seriously, and there was very little "goofing around," but it was still a break from the regular day.

There was one day that did frighten me. We were studying arithmetic, not my favorite subject. In fact, I was staring out the window (my defense when not understanding what was going on in the classroom) when the siren went off. All children were to stay in school for the air raid drill, but if the air raid was real, some children went home based on parent request. While most of us were lead into the hall, as usual, we saw some children put on their coats and leave. This seemed more serious than usual.

Next we heard the roar of bombers overhead. They were loud and we covered our ears. It seemed we were sitting in the hall longer than usual, but suddenly the "all clear" sounded and we went back to the classroom and continued our day.

At the time I thought it was a false alarm. As an adult, reading history of this time, I learned that a Japanese submarine exchanged fire with the Standard Oil tanker, William H. Berg, just off the coast of northern California. It was almost within sight of Half Moon Bay, south and east of the Farallon Islands. Not learning of this as a child is an example of how well our parents kept scary knowledge from us, and how easy it was. There was no TV then to bring all the graphic details of war into each living room as there is now.

When the sirens went off at night, all the lights were to go out, and black curtains hung on the windows. It was the most fun when I was at my grandmother's beautiful big yellow Victorian house where my cousin Sally and her parents lived. This house seemed like a mansion next to our small one-story house. Sally and I slid down the banister and hid from each other in the walk-in closets that went the whole length of the room. It was fun being there at any time, but being there during air raids added to the fun. As we played in the evening, the siren went off, and Sally and I would race up to her parent's bedroom, push chairs up to the high windows and on tiptoes peer out, watching the lights go out all over town. The most impressive was watching the lights at the San Francisco airport go out. This was magical.

Our grandfather was an air raid warden. His job was to patrol the neighborhood during an air raid drill to make sure everyone's lights were off and dark curtains were up so that no lights could be seen coming from houses. He was very proud of his contribution to the "war effort." He kept very careful track of what was happening on the war front. Every evening he sat in his chair with his feet propped up on a footstool next to the furnace, smoking his pipe and listening to the news with Walter Winchell or the comments of Gabriel Heatter. I can still hear Walter Winchell beginning his broadcast with his rapid fire style, "Good evening Mr. and Mrs. North America and all the ships at sea… let's go to press."

This was the attitude of everyone on the "home front." We were proud to do our part for the "war effort." Patriotism abounded. As children, we collected metal and paper for recycling. I most remember saving tin foil from all kinds of wrappers, particularly gum wrappers. Peeling it apart from the paper wrapper, we crumpled it into a ball. Our school had contests with prizes for the biggest foil ball. I never won such a contest, but I kept trying. There was always competition in the neighborhood over who had the biggest ball. The school collected these balls of foil and sent them to the scrap yards for melting, the metal used in making war machines. We also took our wagon around the neighborhood and collected newspaper.

In school each morning after collecting the milk money for the day the teacher asked who wanted to buy a stamp to go toward a War Bond. These War Bonds helped finance the war. Each stamp cost 10 cents and when we had enough, we could trade the book in for a bond.

My third grade class, taught by Miss Pengalli, participated in a Red Cross project for servicemen stationed overseas. We brought shoe boxes to class and filled each with a bar of Ivory soap, a tooth brush, a pack of Lucky Strike cigarettes, a note pad, a pencil, a pair of socks and a deck of cards. Each box was sent to a serviceman.

Another war effort was "Victory gardens." The government encouraged everyone to conserve food, so that more could go to the troops. My mother always had a vegetable garden, which we depended on for our food, but now it took on even more significance. The garden was an important part of winning the war. As a child, this relationship of garden and winning the war was lost on me, but I knew it was important, so I weeded and watered and continued to help Mother can the fruits and vegetables as I always had.

With the constant concern of a possible attack, Mother kept the back porch cupboards stocked with at least a two-week supply of canned foods. As she used something, she replaced it. A list on the door of the first cupboard allowed her to keep a careful account of what was available. I can see now all those jars of fruits, vegetables and fish I helped her can in the summer and fall all crowded together in the cupboards. She kept a few store bought things, also. Two items I particularly remember are chipped beef and Spam. My father loved creamed chipped beef on toast—not my favorite by any means. I did like fried Spam though. Mother made it special by putting a slice of canned pineapple on top of every slice of Spam. The Spam came in a tin with a key to open it. The chipped beef came in a little glass jar.

Certain foods were rationed during the war, especially meat, sugar and butter. It was at this time that oleomargarine became popular. Butter was not available, or if it was we needed to use the little red tokens or stamps in the War Ration Book, allotted monthly. I think the expense stopped us from buying butter even more than the limited number of stamps. Instead we bought white oleomargarine that came with a packet of yellow coloring. Mother would let me put the margarine in a bowl, dump in the yellow coloring and mix it up with my hands. It was wonderfully messy. The soft mushy margarine squished through my fingers as I attempted to mix the oleo and coloring to an even yellow throughout, making it look like butter. There would be oleo up to my elbows before I was finished. It was as good as finger painting. I grew up liking margarine better than butter. As an adult that changed.

Meat was another item that we had little of during the war, so I grew up on a lot of casseroles, which my father hated, but I loved. My favorites were macaroni and cheese and spaghetti made from scratch—nothing box or bottled in those days. Mother cooked the macaroni, made white sauce, and added good sharp cheddar cheese and herbs. She mixed the sauce and macaroni and put in the oven. It would get very crusty on top, which was my favorite part.

The spaghetti, my father made and with great importance. You would think he was making gourmet French cuisine. Each step had to be done just so. First he used lot of oil to sauté the onion, garlic and celery. He wanted olive oil, but we couldn't afford it. This he cooked with care, especially "don't burn the garlic." Then crumble the hamburger and fry it in a separate pan, never the same pan as the onion, garlic and celery. Drain off the fat (of which there was plenty) and put the meat with the onion, garlic and celery. Next add tomatoes my mother had canned and tomato paste. Last, add the herbs–oregano, thyme, rosemary, sage, and bay leaf. It had to cook for several hours to blend the flavors.

To me it was gourmet! Both macaroni and cheese and spaghetti were company foods. Spaghetti was also a company food when we went to our Maynard grandparents' house for dinner. So I grew up believing that spaghetti was a very special dish. I realize now that it was because what little meat we had had to be stretched to feed many people. My mother became very skilled at making food stretch, since we often had sailors show up for meals unexpectedly.

There were a number of military bases in northern California, so there were service men–especially sailors–on every street corner, restaurant, drugstore and bar. When they had a pass they needed a ride to the "big city," San Francisco.

There were government signs on roads saying, "Give a Serviceman a ride." We saw groups of men in uniform on the side of the road with their thumbs out "hitching a ride." My dad always stopped and as many men as possible piled into the car. We even picked up men who were not in uniform. There was no fear at that time of "hitch hikers." In spite of the war, or because of it, it felt like a safe time here at home. It was a time in which we were united and working together to win the war. That was my experience.

It was not the experience of minority groups. I was not aware that many people saw African American men as untrustworthy or that the military did not allow them to serve in the same units as white men, even though they fought hard and distinguished themselves in battle. I knew nothing of the horrible experiences of the Japanese Americans, especially on the west coast. I grew up in a small town just south of San Francisco, where it was illegal for a minority to stay overnight. The place that housed the Japanese Americans until the government sent them to one of the internment camps was less than ten miles from our house, yet I knew nothing. I knew nothing of any of this until I was a young adult and encountered people who had experienced these things.

My mother's cousin Ralph was one of the sailors stationed in the Bay Area, and when given a weekend pass hitched a ride. Often his destination was our house, with one or two of his buddies, looking for a good home-cooked meal. In spite of the fact that we had very little money, my mother always put together a good meal and made it stretch to feed whoever showed up.

It helped that she worked in a grocery store and the owner, a good friend, gave her produce that was a little past its prime and cuts of meat that had not sold. Our house was very small, but the sailors were not fussy. They were just glad for a place to spend the weekend. They slept on the couch or the floor or even the living room chair. My brother Richard and I looked forward to Ralph coming. He most often brought with him his best buddy whose name was also Ralph. Mother's cousin was very tall and his buddy was very short, so we called them big Ralph and little Ralph.

Often we awakened on Saturday morning and there they were, having come in late the night before and sacked out on the living room floor. As we ran to greet them, they would pick us up and twirl us around in the air and then empty their pockets of candy and gum. It was great fun. I am sure spending time with our family helped with their loneliness.

I did not feel any personal sadness related to the war. My father was not drafted nor was the only uncle I knew at that point in my life. My father was extremely underweight and had asthma. He also worked for the State Department of Health on mosquito abatement and malaria. I have a letter his boss wrote to the draft board stating that for all three reasons they should not draft him. He was classified "4F". My uncle Wendell was also "4F." My cousin said it was because he worked for Fairbanks Morse and made things for the war. I suspect it was because he wore glasses.

My father's sensitivity about not going to war makes me think he felt guilty. I think that is why he agreed to let my mother's sister Edna live with us when her husband went off to war. Her husband George was in the army when she met him and they became engaged. They did not plan on marrying right away but suddenly told that his unit was leaving for "overseas," they had a quick marriage. I did not know him or even meet him until the war was over, so I felt no loss at his going. Quick marriages were often the case with young couples during the war.

The radio and the newsreels were important means of communicating what was happening on the war front. When we went to the movies, there was always first the newsreel, then the cartoon, and then the main feature. The newsreel showed men in foxholes and war planes flying and bombs dropping. What I remember most is the sound of bombs dropping. It was a loud screaming noise that started out very high pitched and decreased in pitch as it got closer to earth, and then a big explosion.

There are some fireworks that make that sound today and every time I hear them I cringe. Another sound that makes me shudder is an undulating siren. I don't remember what that sound was during the war, but it came from those newsreels and had a profound effect on me that can cause me to physically react seventy years later. I think about how I see and hear recent wars in far more detail on TV and they don't have as much effect on me. Why? Is it because I was a child at the time, or is it because that kind of horror is coming in to my home nightly with the news? I don't know.

This war was a time of unity for a majority of this country and for me, as a child of six to ten years of age, filled with fun activities and a feeling of safety. It is now seventy Mallorcan years later and men who fought that war are telling their stories, many for the first time. They are painful stories of horror and sadness, so different from my story. Yet my story is as valid as theirs. War is like that – horror stories, but happy ones, too. .

TRAVEL

Great travel writing consists of equal parts curiosity, vulnerability and vocabulary. It is not a terrain for know-it-alls or the indecisive. The best of the genre can simply be an elegant natural history essay, a nicely writ sports piece, or a well-turned profile of a bar band and its music. A well-grounded sense of place is the challenge for the writer. We observe, we calculate, we inquire, we look for a link between what we already know and what we're about to learn. The finest travel writing describes what's going on when nobody's looking.

— Tom Miller

Mallorcan Stone Millhouse Home

MALLORCAN MAELSTROM[17]

By Judy Wydick

At the end of our last sabbatical in 2002, we spent April and May in Mallorca, 90 miles off the coast of Spain. On the internet, Dick had found the perfect place for us to live—in a small canyon outside the village of Aláro in a 300-year-old stone millhouse converted into a home, water fed from an aqueduct built by the Moors a thousand years before. This would be a romantic interlude where Dick could write in solitude—and his high school Spanish would help us through the language issue.

We arrived on a lovely, warm Monday. Our first three days, which began inauspiciously, would show us that simply living there would be a full time job.

The next day the temperature dropped with a thud, and it rained all day. The stone house was stone cold, but when Dick tried to turn on a butane heater, he found the tanks all empty. There was no wood for a fire, and the woods surrounding us were soaked. He tried to phone people designated to help, but he couldn't make the phone work. We managed to find a market (a major chore in itself in the pouring rain) and stock up on food (packaged foods were impossible unless there were pictures), but we really needed warmth. In our first interchanges, we learned that Dick's Spanish didn't prepare him to understand Mallorcan (a dialect of Catalan), and no villagers we met spoke English.

On Wednesday when the house cleaner called to check on us, she explained that you must begin each local phone call with 971, the island code—a vital detail not mentioned in the direction book. She then explained that the local shop where one orders butane tanks is open only on Tuesdays (yesterday), but she told us where we could find some in Palma, 40 miles away. So, during a break in the rain, off we went in our rental car—with me on the map and six empty tanks in the trunk.

Each time Dick stopped, they would roll together hard, so he pulled over to rearrange them. Putting the car in park, he got out, leaving his door open; but he had no sooner exited than the car began to roll forward toward a busy cross-street. I frantically got my leg over the transmission to the brake; and as he rushed back, I hit the brake, which caused his door to close—just as he leaned in. The top corner of the door caught him in the face, and why he didn't lose any teeth, we'll never know. He sat quietly until the blood stopped flowing, fixed the tanks, and we were off again.

We found the address in Palma, but it wasn't a butane outlet! I went to a nearby internet shop to ask for help, and a young man gallantly tried to show me on a street map where we might find the right shop. I went back to tell Dick, when a man walked by carrying a butane tank. Dick ran after him, only to find he was simply *delivering* it! The man made a futile attempt to describe how to reach the butane shop, then motioned for us to follow him in our car.

The man drove quite fast through the city while I madly tried to keep track on the map, but couldn't because of infrequent street signs. Perhaps 20 minutes later, just outside the city, we saw it. And when Dick tried to tip the man, he just smiled, tipped his hat and wouldn't take anything.

Grateful for the help, Dick quickly got full tanks, but then we didn't know where we were so we could get back home! (A map is useless if you do not know your location!) Nearby was a car dealership where I was sure someone could speak English, but no such luck. I did indicate to a young woman that I needed directions to Aláro, however, and with gestures and simple words, she somehow made it clear. On a completely different, but quite beautiful, route, we returned directly to Aláro, thankful that we had accomplished the task.

That night the storm returned with a vengeance, wind howling and rain pounding on the windows, but we were warm! The next day, however, the first floor of our house was flooded (water pouring through the back wall), the deep "dry" ditch along the property had become a raging stream, and the road past our house was a veritable river. A series of phone calls established that everyone's home was flooding and that we were on our own. Dick bailed out over 100 gallons of water before he realized that far more was coming in and that bailing was useless.

What turned out to be the worst storm in generations did subside, and the house finally dried out. Over the next eight weeks we encountered similar challenges, both cultural and physical, in what turned out to be our most memorable sabbatical ever. But from then on, at the very least, we stayed warm!

THE THANKSGIVING CAT[18]

By Elli Norris

Time to go to the ranch,
　another Thanksgiving with Mom at hand,
　turkey, purchased frozen, safe in the fridge.

And there was Lucky, too, dear old cat
　dead for weeks now, frozen, safe in the fridge.
Time to pack the ice chest to go.

Oops! Small oversight. One ice chest, one cat, one turkey.
Well, Lucky first, shrouded in newspapers and plastic.
Next layer, Thanksgiving turkey.

And so we traveled, cat and turkey and me,
　through the valleys and over the hills,
　all the way home for Thanksgiving.

Lucky went into the pet cemetery.
Turkey went into the oven and onto the table.

Wish I'd told Mom. She'd have laughed too.

OUR TURKISH WEDDING[19]

By Jan Smyth

I.   BUYING THE NECKLACE

Our son's fiancé, Yesim, and her brother, Yetkin, had planned to have a double wedding for many years. In the meantime they both moved to the U.S., and married here; however Yesim and her family needed a Turkish wedding to solemnize their joining for themselves and all their Turkish relatives.

Yesim planned the wedding and the surrounding events with her American family and visitors in mind. We were told by Yesim's mother that we must come to represent Sean's family.

Once we decided to attend, we invited our close friends, Char and Paul Bushue, to join us. They were thrilled, and we started making plans. They began their trip in Seattle, while we flew from San Francisco. We met in Istanbul and enjoyed sightseeing there and near Ephesus before heading to Mersin, Yesim's hometown, located in Southern Turkey on the Mediterranean.

There were several wedding events, beginning with Chocolate Night –*kiz isteme* – asking for the blessing. Before this happened we needed to shop for a gold necklace for Yesim, to be presented at the formal wedding, the culmination of all the wedding activities.

We arrived in Mersin, Turkey on June 17th, 2009. The next morning, Yesim and Sean came to our room at the hotel and the four of us went downstairs to the lobby to greet her parents, Zubeyde and Nurettin. We knew them already, as they had visited us in the United States. We visited for a while, and then we asked them to explain what was going to happen at the "Chocolate Party" that evening.

Zubeyde explained and Yesim translated. The tradition was for the groom's parents to arrive at their home with the silver tureen,

---

which Yesim bought for us at the Grand Bazaar in Istanbul. This tureen is shaped a little like the base of Aladdin's lamp, only the top is open like a bowl. Nurettin and Zubeyde said they were having it filled with fine chocolates and would give it to us when they picked us up that evening. We would present it to Yesim and her family when we arrived at their home. It really was our responsibility to fill it, but we didn't realize that at the time.

Zubeyde continued: after meeting and visiting with the family members, one of us must ask formally for Yesim to join our family. Zubeyde told us what to say and I wrote it down. They briefly described the rest of the evening. Originally it was supposed to be just the six of us, but Zubeyde warned us that others might come. It turned out all the aunts, uncles, cousins and friends that were nearby had asked to be there too. Zubeyde said everyone was curious about the American family Yesim was joining. We later learned that in Turkey friends and relatives feel free to come to any event they hear about, invited or not. This makes it very difficult for the person planning any event.

After taking notes, we realized we needed to leave for the jewelry store to buy the necklace. We took a taxi from our hotel, and told the driver to follow Nurettin's car to the jewelry store in downtown Mersin. Yesim, her mother and Sean rode with Nurettin. The jewelry store was owned by the man whose father taught Nurettin the jewelry trade.

Jewelry stores in Turkey sell different size gold coins attached to a ribbon and a small safety pin. These gold coins range in price from $1/4^{th}$ to 1 Turkish lira. The price fluctuates daily based on the price of gold. Currently one lira is about $65. Instead of buying kitchen or home gifts as we do in the U.S., friends and family will buy one of these gold coins, which they will pin onto the bride or groom during the wedding celebration. After the wedding, the couple is expected to return them to the jewelry store and redeem them for cash. Close family members may give a piece of gold jewelry. As the groom's parents we were expected to buy a gold necklace and perhaps a bracelet.

Nurettin told the owner we were looking for jewelry for the wedding. They began bringing out trays with gold chains and necklaces. There was no jewelry displayed inside the store, but obviously much in the back of the store. Yesim and I quickly agreed on two large and one larger coin to be placed on a broad gold chain. They put the chain around her neck, and she indicated where it should be cut for the length. They also brought out some gold bracelets. After some time we chose one we both liked.

This all took quite a while, as near the beginning of the selection process, Nurettin looked out the front window of the store and saw the police were about to give him a ticket. He ran out and was able to keep the police from towing it away; however he had to drive quite a distance to find a legal parking spot and then walk all the way back. This took about twenty minutes. While he was gone we were served our choice of soft drinks or tea and visited.

When Nurettin returned the serious negotiations began. Finally a price was given and by the look on her parents' faces and tone of voice, I knew they thought it was too much. Yesim told us the price, and said she thought it was more than we had planned to spend. When we heard the price, I'm sure our expressions showed our shock. We agreed that we could only afford a little less than half of the price given. Nurettin negotiated some more, the bracelet was removed and the chain of the necklace, shortened slightly. A small gold coin for Henna night was added, and the price was agreed on.

Once we knew the price, Don gave them his American Express card. They said they needed a pin and we all said "no", in unison, as that meant it was going to be a debit. We gave our Visa card and eventually that went through.

After the purchase we were to go to the jewelry store owned by Nurettin's brother, which was around the corner. Zubeyde and Nurettin planned to purchase the wedding rings for Yesim and Sean there; however, because Nurettin had been gone so long to park the car we were quite late.

As it was lunchtime, we changed plans and went to lunch first. We walked about two blocks to a small café on a walkway with no cars. There were tables inside and out. As it was a beautiful day, we sat outside under some trees. Nurettin ordered for all of us. Lunch consisted of thinly sliced rotisserie lamb served over fresh cubed bread, similar in texture to bagels. A large helping of yogurt was also on the plate and a thick tomato-based sauce was placed on the table, which we poured onto the lamb. It was delicious!

Nurettin, Zubeyde, Sean, Yesim, Don & Jan

Zubeyde and Nurettin were quite distressed, as they had planned to take us to an upscale restaurant; however, it would have taken too long to retrieve the car, drive to lunch and then come back to the other jewelry store for them to buy the rings. We kept telling them how much we enjoyed the lunch, but they insisted on taking us to lunch the following day at the nicer restaurant.

By the time we finished eating, we knew we needed to get back to the hotel for a rest before we formally met the bride's extended family for the first time later. Don and I taxied back to the hotel and Sean, Yesim and her folks went to buy the rings.

Don and I talked before stretching out for a rest. Other than our original shock and embarrassment at the cost of Turkish jewelry, we had enjoyed ourselves thoroughly and were learning so much about the customs. We both looked forward to the gathering in the evening and meeting more of Yesim's extended family.

II. THE CHOCOLATE PARTY
(*kiz isteme, or blessing*)

Sean and one of Yesim's many uncles picked us up at our hotel that evening to take us to the Chocolate Party. We were ushered into the backseat of a pickup. The leg room was so tight that by the time we arrived Don was so stiff that getting out was difficult.

When we arrived at their home, Yesim, Zubeyde and Nurettin greeted us. We entered the living room and two more uncles, two aunts, four cousins and a few others came up to meet us. Fortunately one cousin, Shenar, studied in the U.S. for four years, so when Yesim left the room he could translate. If they both were out of the room, we all smiled a lot.

We sat down in their large formal living/dining room with many traditional chairs upholstered in off-white, antique furniture, a huge dining room table and two cabinets. One cabinet contained a collection of silver and the other, crystal.

After visiting a little, Yesim's uncle and Yesim gestured to the effect, "Let's get this show on the road". Then I looked at the note I had written that morning when Zubeyde told me what to say. I formally asked her parents if, with God's permission and their blessing, Yesim could marry Sean and become part of our family. There was a pause, and then one of her uncles said the family would think about it and we could come back in a year for the wedding. Everyone laughed. Another uncle asked Sean how often he would bring Yesim to visit them in Turkey. Sean didn't know what to say, so Yesim whispered, "Say once a year, it doesn't matter." Sean did, and everyone said "Ah," or sighed with relief and smiled .

Then Zubeyde said how impressed they were with Sean, what good manners he had, and that they were happy because they knew their daughter would always be cared for, even in poor health. She went on to say it was clear how well he had been raised, and that it made it easier for them, with Yesim living so far away, to know that she would be with such a caring husband and family. All the women, including Yesim and I became teary (I think some of the men too). It brought home to me how very difficult it was for them to see their daughter move so far away.

Earlier Yesim asked me to go out of the room with her, where she gave me two rings that she had been wearing for some time, but were new to her family and would therefore count as engagement rings. I was to give one to Don and the other to Sean after the two families had agreed to the marriage. They then placed the rings on her finger, and everyone clapped.

Following this engagement ceremony, Don and I were seated. Then Yesim took my hand, put her forehead to it, and then kissed it. She then did the same with Don, followed by Sean repeating the gesture. Following this, pictures were taken, coffee or drinks were served, and Yesim passed around the large oval silver tureen, now filled with elaborately-wrapped fancy chocolates. There was even one packaged with two chocolates and the image of a bride and groom on the outside of the wrapping, similar to the designs we often see on the top of wedding cakes.

Eventually, after the coffee and chocolates, the table was set and we were all, about thirteen, seated at the large table. Food was brought in in abundance, all sorts of Turkish courses, including *borek*, which is one of my favorites (similar to the Greek *spanokopita*), and many dishes that we tried for the first time.

As mentioned earlier, this meeting was supposed to be small but family and neighbors kept arriving to meet us. When we were about through eating another couple, who were lifelong friends arrived. Even Sean's cousin Sarah, whose flight was late, arrived. Zubeyde asked latecomers to join us, they declined, she insisted, and plates were brought.

Following dinner the table was cleared and we all went back to sit in the living room area. A large platter of baklava was brought in and set on a separate small table. One of the cousins began putting two or three pieces on small plates, and Yesim and others served all the guests.

When all were served, Sean and Yesim were given one plate with three or four pieces. An uncle told Sean he must put one whole square in his mouth at once. He did and everyone clapped and laughed. Yesim's uncle said that doing this showed Sean would not speak too much in their marriage. (Another big group laugh.) Then Yesim fed one to Sean, and Sean to Yesim.

After this was finished and everyone had eaten their baklava, we said it was time for us to leave. We thanked her family and said our goodbyes. Nurettin and Sean drove us back to the hotel. I did notice that as soon as we started to leave, some of the others were also preparing to depart.

Back in our room, after a very long day, we both agreed that this wedding experience was well worth the long flight, and would probably become one of our most memorable trips.

Jan, Don and Sean at Chocolate Night

III. HENNA NIGHT/COUNTRY WEDDING

There were several wedding events, but one of the most memorable was the Henna Night/Country Wedding celebration. Yesim's Henna Night was not a traditional one, as men were invited. She combined the country wedding celebration and Henna Night. Yesim did this because the American visitors had a limited time they could stay in Turkey. Usually Henna Night occurs earlier than the country wedding, with a huge gathering of women relatives and friends.

Yesim therefore added many of the Henna night customs to the Country Wedding Ceremony. She and Becky wore the traditional costumes, the Turkish dancers and singers from a regional dance company came in their native costumes, and the music consisted of three drums and a clarion, a large horn. There was a ceremony with henna, but unlike the traditional Henna Night, both grooms sat with their future brides, during the ceremony.

The chartered bus came to our hotel and fourteen wedding guests boarded about 5:30 p.m. We wove slowly through the busy downtown Mersin streets to the Kurtulus residence (Yesim and Yetkin's parents).

Sean, some of the household helpers, neighbors and friends boarded, as well as guests staying at the Kurtulus' beach house on the Mediterranean, outside of town. Every seat on the bus was occupied. The bus continued to the outskirts of town, where we picked up the dance performers, who had to stand in the aisle. From Mersin we traveled to the nearby farm community of Kazanli, where Yesim's family has owned a large farm for many generations.

The bus driver parked at the entrance to the farm. As we walked down a long gravel driveway, three drummers greeted us, beating out a loud slow beat. They continued playing as they followed us up the driveway. Lambs turned on spits to the left of the driveway as we walked. When we reached the farm house on the right, ahead of us were long decorated tables set up to hold all the side dishes. Yesim's Mother, Zubeyde, greeted everyone as they arrived.

The festivities had not begun, but we noticed some people had found the soft drinks and beer in ice filled buckets, so we helped ourselves to drinks, found a place at the tables to sit and waited ….and waited. Yesim later explained that her uncle, who was supposed to bring the tables, hadn't arrived with them until late in the afternoon, so when Yesim and her family should have been getting dressed, they were still setting up tables. (Even when we were in Istanbul Yesim had worried about the haphazard way things were often done in Turkey. When she called her mother in Mersin to check on progress, Yesim couldn't get a clear answer; Zubeyde had just told her to get there as soon as possible to check on the plans.)

Eventually a car drove partway up the long driveway bringing the brides. The grooms, Sean and Yetkin, walked to the car as the three drummer moved along behind them, beating loudly on their instruments. Sean and Yetkin helped Becky and Yesim get out of the car, as the brides were dressed in the traditional Turkish outfits, including slippers that didn't fit too well, balloon pants and decorated tops with lots of gold trim. Yesim's costume was a redish orange, and Becky's, deep purple. The couples walked slowly up the driveway, again accompanied by loud drumbeats.

By the time the lamb and rice were ready and being served, the long table had been filled with many Turkish dishes brought by family, neighbors and friends. We went to the table and helped ourselves to an array of foods, including luscious fresh tomatoes, cucumbers and watermelon. The hot dishes were varied, but used many common Turkish favorites; *berek,* a pastry filled with a variety of vegetables and/or meats, zucchini stuffed in a tomato-based mixture of meat, herbs and spices, and several dishes with eggplant. Servers brought the roasted meat and rice on separate plates.

When we finished eating, the musicians came to the tables, played the clarion right in our ears, and expected to be given money to go away. This is a tradition, even though the family also pays them. Finally, near the end of the evening Yesim's father noticed the musicians counting their money, saw how much they had collected, and told them to stop!

Sean and Yesmin

Yesmin and Zubeyde

. The core ceremony of Henna Night or "Kina Gecesi" was included, but instead of holding this ceremony at the beginning of the evening it occurred much later, following the meal, performance of the dancers and some dancing by guests.

Yesim and Becky were seated at a small table. Sean sat beside Yesim and Yetkin, next to Becky. A veil was placed over the head of each bride, symbolizing the bride's tears. Next women with candles set in henna-filled dishes walked around them and sang some traditional songs.

Henna was put into the palms of the brides hands; one of the women closed their hands over the henna. They weren't supposed to open their hands until their mothers-in-law placed a gold coin in their palm. Now I understood the reason for the gold coin that we purchased earlier, along with a gold necklace.

The henna represents fertility and the gold coin to bring wealth or good fortune in their new life. Usually the bride's hands are covered with a red cloth glove for the entire celebration, but Yesim and Becky refused to do this. The bridegrooms had henna placed on their little fingers, after which a handkerchief was wrapped around the henna and around their wrists. Sean and Yetkin didn't keep this on after the ceremony, either.

When the henna ceremony was almost completed, Yesim's cousin, Levent, came and warned us that there were going to be blank shots fired from a pistol. Yesim's uncle Yusuf shot a pistol in the air 6 times. (When we asked the significance of the 6 shots, Yesim said she thought it was just because that is what that weapon held. As to why he shot the gun, she didn't know and just referred to "tradition".)

Following the henna ceremony, the dancing continued, but soon I told Sean we needed to leave. Some of the others were leaving also, and Sean helped me walk back to the bus, while Don told our friends Char and Paul, who decided to stay until the evening was over.

When Don and I were seated along with a few other couples, the dance group boarded the bus and rode back into town with us. As the bus headed toward Mersin, the dancers sang songs and played one of their instruments in the background. Their serenade was a lovely way to end our evening.

The next day Sean's cousin Mary asked Yesim if her mother would explain what the various Henna Night rituals symbolized. Zubeyde replied she didn't know, but suggested Mary "Google" it. We all laughed, as it reminded us that we would have a hard time explaining the reasons for many of our traditions, as well.

GRANDMA'S HOMESTEAD[20]

By Nancy Maynard

It was September 1994. Carol and I were hot and tired and almost out of gas when we drove into Williston. It looked like an interesting little town on the North Dakota prairie. We stopped at a gas station, filled up the camper and asked where we could find the county court house. "Just a quarter of a mile on down the street on your right", the attendant said.

Sure enough, there it was, a big stone imposing looking building with grass and trees around it. Just what a county court house should look like. We parked across the street in the parking lot and read the historical marker telling us that "The Old Red Brick Williams County Courthouse" stood where the parking lot is now. It was built in 1899. This would have been the building where my grandmother filed on her homestead in 1906. Now it is a parking lot. What would she think if she could be here now?

We crossed the street to the new courthouse and easily found the signs directing us to the registrar of deeds. Oh, I hope he can direct us to that property that was once hers. A very friendly man behind the desk labeled "Registrar of Deeds—Jim Evans" greeted us. "Can I help you?" I told him what I wanted and his face lit-up. "Yes, I would be glad to help you." The joy and expectation in his voice told me it was something he enjoyed doing and I was not the first person to come in with this request.

I gave him the official location of the land, West ½ of the Northeast ¼ and the West ½ of the Southeast ¼, Section 26, in Township 156, North of Range 102, West of the Principal Meridian. He pulled out a map showing all the townships and sections with all the present day roads. Then he colored in the piece of land that was my grandmother's homestead and drew on the map exactly how to get there.

"After you turn this last corner," he said, "in about a quarter of a mile you will see a ditch or a fence. That will be the beginning of the property." He knew the county like the back of his hand and loved to share his knowledge with those who were interested. Next he gave me a copy of my grandmother's deed to the homestead and showed me all the names of the people who had owned it since my grandmother. He also made copies of some of the history of Cow Creek Township, which is where this property is located.

It was obvious that he was having as much fun finding these documents as I was in receiving them and reveled in my excitement. As we went out the door, loaded down with all this information and thanking him profusely, he said, "Now don't be disappointed. You won't find anything there but a wheat field. The old sod houses have all been torn down. They were a hazard and often in the way of planting."

Off we went, with great excitement. We followed his directions with the map, and sure enough, when we turned the corner and went about a quarter of a mile, there was a ditch. I stopped the camper and just looked. This was it! This is where my grandmother built her sod house and lived for fourteen months, much of the time by herself. This is the land she "proved up." It was just flat prairie with a slight rise to the north, and a few trees way off in the west.

I got out and walked around. It was just a field with wheat stubble now. As I walked around, picking up a few rocks, I thought about her and the stories she wrote about her experiences here.

Once coming from a trip to town, she got lost in a blizzard. After wandering around in circles for hours and listening to the wolves howling, and sure she would freeze to death or the wolves would get her, she gave her horse free rein and soon he stopped in front of the "shanty." It was 3 A.M.

She wrote about keeping her meat in a snow bank during the day, but having to bring it in at night to keep the wolves from getting it. Another story she told was about the joy of skiing on a frosty morning. What an adventurer she must have been!

I thought about the picture of her standing in front of her sod house in her long skirt, white long-sleeved blouse, and hat, as though she were about to go to a fancy affair. Then I looked down at my jeans and blue denim shirt. What a difference.

How did she live here, in the middle of nowhere, in a sod house, and do all she had to do in a long skirt and white blouse? And what need did she have of a hat? What would she have thought of me in my jeans and camper if I had pulled up to her sod house for a visit?

Annie Marguerite Jacaobson Iddings 1906

Nancy Maynard 1994

Recollecting Myself...[21]

By Elli Norris

I seem to have abandoned
    parts of myself,
Left them strewn across the landscape
    of my history.

Now is the time to journey home over its geography,
    sifting and choosing
Recollecting some lost, new-discovered parts,
Leaving others to molder and seep into my soil
To nourish seeds of New Beginnings.

Thanksgiving Day, 1995. The Ranch.

Steward... and Lover[22]

By *Elli Norris*

In Spanish 'la querencia' refers to a place on the ground where one feels secure, a place from which one's strength of character is drawn... [It is] a place in which we know exactly who we are. The place from which we speak our deepest beliefs.

Barry Lopez. *The Rediscovery of North American.*
University Press of Kentucky, Lexington, KY. 1990.

I know such a place. It lies in the rolling oak woodlands of the Southern Sierra, Tulare County, and it was home to the Native People for thousands of years, then to first white settlers who came in the 1860s and onward, and, since 1928, to my grandparents, my parents, and finally, to me. Even though I no longer live on that land, it still lives in my heart and it continues to be the place from which I speak my deepest beliefs—when I take courage. This is the story of the ranch, and of the dream that came true during the years I lived there as an adult, after Mother died and it came to me.

I was imprinted by this land at birth. Like one of Konrad Lorenz's baby geese, I emerged from the darkness, fixed my eyes upon these gentle rolling hills and meadows, and fell in love. Although I have

---

traveled far away, always it has been here to welcome me home, and now, at last, I have returned to stay.

In truth, I did not gaze upon this particular land in my first moments or even first weeks of life, for I was born in the small agricultural community of Porterville, 25 miles away in the flatlands of California's San Joaquin Valley. But this is true —s presence permeated the very walls of my inner home those nine months of growing and the months of early awareness in the outer world. My earliest memories are of climbing into the old maroon Ford, 1930s vintage, to head for the distant hills to visit Grandma and Grandpa, but most of all, to visit The Ranch.

How far 25 miles are for a 4-year-old, at first sitting in the back seat behind Mom and Dad, but soon leaning over the front seat, and beginning the litany, "How far is it now? How much farther?" Always the response, "Just around the next corner," until finally it <u>was</u> just around the next corner and there, wondrously spread before us, was the rutted driveway curving onward from county road, and the barn. Huge, to a child, and still huge today. Big, old, open hay barn, and its weathered beams and shake roof formed a piece with the grassy field from which it grew.

Later, an adolescent, I helped Grandpa and Dad heave flakes of sweet-smelling hay into the feeding troughs in winter for the rough-coated red Herefords. "Ho, beevies," I learned to say softly, like my grandpa, soothing them. Today, now that the barn and all its environs have passed from Grandpa to Mother to me, it is still a big barn. Its shake roof has turned to corrugated iron, but the wooden siding and posts still stand sturdy. The smell of hay once stored here is only a memory, yet the ghosts of grandfather and father and my own younger self are here.

So many ghosts walk this land. Ghosts of white settlers, ghosts of those far older than they. It was probably the Yaudanchi who came here, a clan of the vast Yokuts tribe which had filled California's Great Central Valley until the Spaniards and then the Americans came. These native people had a village here, just beyond the barn, maybe a few hundred of them making their living off the land. Just outside my door are granite boulders pocked with worn acorn grinding holes. A large mortar of reddish stone and its pestle, turned up when Dad was hunting rocks for a garden wall years ago, lie nearby. Obsidian chips work their way up out of the soil after a rain. Just the other day I caught the glitter of something in the dirt and, bending down, came up with a perfect, tiny arrowhead.

I walk back over the land, eyes searching jumbled boulders for more signs: a petroglyph, a pictograph? No, not that, but the spring which once satisfied the thirst of those Indians, and which, from the 1850s on into the 1900s, became a regular stopping place for white settlers passing by, still spills out today beside the house to fill a cup and water a garden.

The valley and blue and live oaks were extravagant with their yield in the days gone by. The harvest of acorns was a staple in the Indian diet. And *brodiaea* – those early people made ample harvest of their bulbs, digging in fields of purple-blue and pink and yellow and white blooms to find "little potatoes" to add to their diet. The Yokuts, like tribes throughout California, cultivated the earth with their digging sticks, taking plenty, leaving plenty to multiply for next year's crop.

What am I to this land? How shall I call myself? Steward? Caretaker? Am I tender of the land, taking care to harvest and plant in harmony with the needs of this particular place? Perhaps I am an at-tender. Attending to the rhythms of this earth as to those of a lover.

Lover. Oh yes, surely that is what I am to this land, and it to me. Is it too late? Can I attune myself again to the messages encoded in my own being and know myself as a lover with this land? Can I walk in the footsteps of those who came before me, learn to harvest little potatoes in springtime and acorns in the fall, help this earth do what it knows how to do, make more?

I know I must try, for it is no small thing to be captured at birth by a land. It has called to me over years and miles, through the very cells of my being. I come home at last and find it, the faithful lover, waiting.

125

November 19, 2013 Note: I wrote this love letter to the land in 1992, the year after I moved home from Berkeley, sure that I would live there for the rest of my life. And yet, 19 years later I left it for a new home in Davis, California. But I had been a good steward and I left it in good hands. In stories that follow in my memoirs, I tell some of the stories of what happened in those 19 years, the dream that came true and that allows cattle and kids to roam its hills now and in perpetuity.

THE LAND SPEAKS[23]

By Elli Norris

I am the Land
   and I abide

I have been wrenched and kneaded,
   cast up to the heights
   and down into the depths.
The waters have burnished my rocky faces
   and carved the deep folds of my ravines.
I am clothed in vibrant green and gold of living things
   and in the stark, sere shades of dust.
I am wilderness
   and I am tamed.

Through all,
   through eons of it all...

   I abide.

Come... I am here.

Silver and Elli Blowing Bubbles at the Grotto

SUMMER EVENINGS[24]

By Elli Norris

Summer evenings at the ranch are long and slow. Sometimes, as now, they bring a fresh breeze, and it's cool enough to come outdoors to sit. Summer evenings don't allow one to stay indoors watching TV. Sacrilege. One must come out, walk a bit, stand and stare, find a good place to sit and stare some more.

Kept company by Silver, my cocker spaniel, I wander down the path behind the house to the grotto I call Gaia's Grotto, after the Earth Mother. I hear the splash of the overflow from the well on the hill above into Gaia's small pool formed by natural granite boulders and the work of a friend eager to create a thing of beauty. I watch the water flow over the rock dam and form a steam between more rocks set out by my friend. The water, cool and just about deep enough to cover my sandaled feet, murmurs quietly onward through the grasses, and away out of sight. Gaia's pool is just "sitting down deep," but tonight I sit on the bench nearby and gaze up through the giant sycamores that blot out the sky with their old, spreading arms, their great canopy of leaves. Silver rustles and snuffles through the leaves in search of lizards or bugs or anything else he might eat.

We move on to another bench, this one set between two giant sycamores beside Gaia's creek. There, on the other side, a great valley oak rises 100 feet into the air (or so it seems), its arms reaching to left and right. Birds live in them all, the oaks, the sycamores, the grasses of the fields. Birds, lizards, insects, snakes, too. I look down at the little stream making its way slowly through the stands of stinging nettle, through the watercress that grows spontaneously on its surface, onward to the great boulders that divide its path and create a small pool where fish idle until enticed by a floating insect meal.

Evening is falling and Silver and I meander to the east deck of the house, which looks up at the Sierra Nevada, an hour's drive but maybe only five miles more or less for one of the turkey vultures who frequent

---

[24] Copright©2014 Eleanor L. Norris

our neighborhood. Standing out against the darkening sky is Moses Mountain, 9,000 feet above sea level, his granite mouth hanging open in an ancient snore. He has come to the mountain top, and here he lies forever. Beyond him, out of sight, I know lies the mountain someone named Maggie, surely not Moses' Biblical wife, but the wife – or girlfriend – of some early-day mountain wanderer struck by the two up-thrust conical ridges of "her" bosom.

The birds have gone to bed now. It's quiet but for the trickle of water from the old spring by the deck and the families of tiny green frogs that live there and loudly sing their evening song. This spring and its burbling waters and singing creatures are friends from my childhood, friends of my parents and grandparents before me, and of the Native Americans before them. It puts out only a trickle now, not enough to supply my house and yard, but enough to add its peaceful sound, to fill a pool, to remind us of what and who has been here before.

Voices now, and I see three people jogging down the county road 100 yards across my front pasture. In the unusual cool of this July evening they jog and chat. In the field between me and them, a doe raises her head from the tall grass, looks around, watches me watching the runners on the county road. Then she melts out of sight, and I wonder if that browner swatch in the golden grass is an ear. Yesterday I saw her in the front meadow grazing, so graceful, and suddenly she squatted. There is something slightly embarrassing about observing such a graceful creature squat to defecate. Straight back, she sinks back on her hind legs, quite modest, to be honest. Yet such an unfamiliar posture for this lovely creature, to the eyes of a human such as I.

Summer evenings are slow. They must be honored outdoors. One must sit quietly and watch, and listen. Silver doesn't sit and watch; he putters about, hoping to find a gopher or field mouse. Too late for a quail. And then he comes to lie down at my feet and watch awhile before rising, wandering off to hunt again. Desultorily.

Mornings are different. They have an urgency about them, at least if I don't get up until 6 or so, an hour before sun-up now, in July.

130

Perhaps if I rose at 5, these quiet, meditative moments would greet me. But at 6, knowing the sun will be up soon and bring its warmth, if not its heat, the new day begins and brings with it tasks, real or imagined. Mornings are not slow. Quiet, yes. And cool and crisp, especially this unusual July with mornings of 50 degrees. Invigorating, and there are things to do before the heat descends like a heavy blanket.

I rise, and Silver and I walk up the old road to the pond, continue on to the "Old Hay Field," so-called since my memory begins, down along Lower Creekside Trail, and stop for a moment at the grove of giant redwoods I call the Mary E. Charlton Memorial Grove. When Mary died in 1995, friends proposed planting redwoods in her honor, and so we did. Five little trees planted from 5-gallon tubs in the small field behind the house. They stand some 12 to 15 feet high now. Will they survive another 25 or 30 or 50 years or more? I hope so, but I won't be around to know.

Silver and I make a detour to Gaia's Grotto to say good morning to Great Mama, and then wander on to the house. I continue my morning rituals – light the candles at my altars, eat a quiet breakfast in the living room where I can look out at the meadow in front of the house, greet Moses beyond, and write some words in my daily journal. Yes, anyone would say, a quiet morning, a slow morning.

But soon I rise and begin the day, take on whatever tasks call to me. Warmth begins to permeate the house, and I close the windows that I had opened last night to let in the cooling air, and to close the blinds against the sun. A ritual of summer. In the morning, close up the house against the heat of the day. Turn on the air conditioning when the heat becomes uncomfortable. In the evening, open up the windows and doors to the fresh cooling air. My mother did it, and her mother before her, and now I do it too.

Summer evenings are for dreaming, for closing up the day and resting, for giving thanks for this land, this earth, my life. But I do that in the morning, too, dream and give thanks. But the morning is for beginnings. The evening is for endings. I give thanks for beginnings. I give thanks for endings.

LIFE GOES ON

The trouble with retirement is that you never get a day off. – Abe Lemons

When a man retires and time is no longer a matter of urgent importance, his colleagues generally present him with a watch – R.C. Sherriff

Old age isn't so bad when you consider the alternative. – Maurice Chevalier

A man's age is something impressive, it sums up his life: maturity reached slowly and against many obstacles, illnesses cured, griefs and despairs overcome, and unconscious risks taken; maturity formed through so many desires, hopes, regrets, forgotten things, loves. A man's age represents a fine cargo of experiences and memories. – Antoine de Saint-Exupery, *Wartime Writings 1939-1944*, translated from French by Norah Purcell.

LIFE GOES ON[25]

By Alouise Hillier

How could life go on when my husband Ken had left with my heart? I searched for comfort by thinking of the happy and contented years that we had had together. I thanked God that Ken didn't have to experience the pain of losing *me*. I read and reread messages of consolation from friends and acquaintances. Cards and notes from URC residents surprised and comforted me.

One new acquaintance quietly expressed her condolences and said, "It gets better, Alouise." She had experienced the same grief the previous year. That gave me the determination to summon the courage to say, "I'm doing well" when asked the automatic question, "How are you?"

I did not now need the extra services and expense of the Assisted Living apartment where we had been living, but I simply could not face another move.

However, after two years, I decided to move to an apartment in Independent Living with the same floor plan. Convinced that we could arrange the available space to enable me to pursue my sewing projects, my daughter Lynn measured the space and then searched for furniture that would meet my needs. We converted the bedroom into a sewing-computer-office and installed a Murphy bed in the living room to be lowered at night. I downsized again, keeping only an antique trunk and platform rocker, the teak dining table, two chairs, and my sewing machine in its spacious cabinet.

The new cabinets and computer desk, lining the walls of both rooms, leave enough space in the center of the sewing room for the drop-leaf work table that had been built for me. The cabinets provide ample storage for my fabric stash and quilting supplies. When I raise the two long leaves of the cutting table, there is scarcely any floor space remaining, but I am thankful for the convenience it provides.

My walls hold small quilted projects that I created while living in New Mexico. Staff and visitors admired my displays and suggested that they be displayed elsewhere in the building. At the request of the Resident Art Committee, Alice Delwiche and I organized a quilt show in which I displayed many items that had won awards at the county and regional fairs of New Mexico and Texas.

Residents urged me to participate in the Yolo County Fair, in which my entries garnered many awards that earned the Senior Citizen's Sweepstakes Award three years in a row. At the nearby Dixon May Fair, my entry of an antique cigar ribbon quilt that I had completed for Fran Hillier won the special award of the Fair Manager's Choice. The elegant stitching in the assembly of silk cigar ribbons had been done by Eleanore Harmon, circa 1925. My contribution was the finishing of the quilt, but because of its novelty the award became mine.

I have found that my friend's comment, "Things will get better," has gradually come true. Martha Maclivane's cheerful encouragement buoyed my jaded spirits. She offered to take me in her car for errands after I gave up my car. One day we drove to Winters, a small town less than 20 miles west of Davis. I shopped in a quilt shop to purchase fabric using a $60 award certificate from the county fair entry.

On our return drive, at the first stop light Martha turned into the left hand lane. I said I thought we should turn right, but she strongly disagreed. Nothing looked familiar to me as we drove out of the small town, but I refrained from commenting for several minutes. However, I finally said that I didn't recognize anything in view. She confessed that she was feeling as confused as I, but instead of turning around, she continued driving on with determination.

Most roads exiting the highway were narrow and not likely to lead us to Davis. Finally, we turned right on a stretch of road that seemed more likely than the former, but we soon discovered that it led only to a small factory with no extension beyond it. So we returned to the main highway. I suggested that we turn left and attempt to find our way back to our starting point, but instead we turned right. How could we be so confused and lost when we knew that we could not be far from Davis? We continued for approximately seven or eight miles, when we finally saw a road leading to Esparto. I realized that we had traveled north and now were west of Woodland. Since I had driven to Woodland several times before I gave up my car, I suddenly became oriented and could confidently give the directions back to familiar territory.

Our laughter over that ridiculous incident cemented a friendship that we enjoyed for eight years. We did not spend a great deal of time together, but each meeting was a special joy. She helped me in so many ways. I could reciprocate by offering my sewing skills when needed.

My troublesome left knee worsened and caused me to limit many of my usual activities, such as long walks and visits to museums that required much standing. I enjoyed good health, so at age 89, I decided to have a knee replacement.

The surgery was successful, but I could not tolerate the pain medication, oxycontin, which caused panic attacks. I suffered a long and slow recovery, which finally became alleviated by acupuncture treatments and expert care from Alzada Magdalena, a highly skilled technician. I finally realized that the extreme pain was caused by the muscles that were readjusting to the realignment of the knee.

Meanwhile, Martha was losing her battle with breast cancer. I couldn't go to visit her mainly because of my fear of panic attacks, but she bravely came to say farewell to me. I lost my dear friend on December. 28, 2009. I felt so emotionally unbalanced that I could not attend her memorial service.

137

I grieved for Martha as I slowly regained my physical and mental health. One day I realized that I no longer had the fear of panic. Martha had helped me even in her death. Yes, life does go on.

MARTHA[26]

By Alouise Hillier

December 30, 2008

Martha died today.
She was my first friend and acquaintance here at URC.
We're old. Our precious friendships are of short duration.

Martha, thank you for your comfort in my grieving.

Martha, I've fallen. Does my bleeding brow
   need more than a band aid?
Martha, will you help me identify the acrid smell
   coming from next door in the middle of the night?
Martha, I'm grieving for your illness, but my slow recovery
   from surgery, overmedication, and panic attacks
   prevent me from coming to you.

How very brave you were to come to me to say farewell.
With your son at your side you eschewed the
   wheelchair and walked to my apartment.

Martha, thank you.
My heart hears your reply, "It gives me pleasure."

EPILOGUE

Strangely, grieving has quelled my fear of panic.
I'm getting well.

THE BUILDING PROJECT[27]

By Alouise Hillier

Construction of the new addition to the north wing of URC began in February 2010. The project started with the digging of a hole for the basement parking garage. The day the heavy equipment began arriving, I watched in wonder to see large mechanical objects and tools for the first time. One strange-looking self-propelled object parked itself. Then, slowly, its arms and legs began to unfold and spread out, creating a sturdy base for the huge shovel that soon rose into the air, to be used to remove trailer loads of soil.

The shovel had large sharp teeth, which bit into the soil that had been loosened by a small tractor and shovel. Filled with a huge scoopful, it swung around to dump the load into a waiting trailer-truck.. Four full scoops filled the long trailer in about five minutes. As the filled trailer-truck moved away, another took its place to be filled. One hundred loads were removed every day for six days.

I wondered where all the good soil was deposited after leaving URC. To my amusement, Ruth Wildman satisfied my curiosity by following a truck, which led to the field of a farm several miles northwest of Davis. There she saw a load being dumped onto the mounds of soil that had accumulated with each truckload. She surmised that it would be used as fill to level low areas in the field.

Day by day I watched and marveled, developing an appreciation of the operator's skill in manipulating the heavy equipment. Down in the growing hole, the operator of the little tractor moved it around nimbly and swiftly, often turning its nose up at a sharp angle to climb an embankment that was created as the hole grew deeper by the removal of the soil. I watched in awe, amazed that the little tractor always stayed upright.

---

[27] Copyright©2014 Alouise Hillier

141

URC addition under construction   Photo by Wes Yates

Fortunately the noisy dusty activity fascinated me as I watched a safe distance away. But many residents, whose apartments were closer to the working area than mine, had difficulty enduring the shrill beeping and loud motor noises, as tractors and trucks moved back and forth seven to eight ceaseless hours each day, which started promptly at seven o'clock.

I often watched at an open window at the end of the hall, where I could poke my head out to observe the men making preparations for other phases of the construction. I was perfectly safe, but that was naturally viewed as an unsafe activity, so I reluctantly resisted, not wishing to cause alarm for my safely.

The work progressed through the months, with different crews and different equipment for the tasks as they proceeded with the construction. At well-attended monthly meetings, the project foreman entertained and informed us about the progress and upcoming schedules.

I thought I had seen big cranes until the BIG one moved in to lift beams, walls, and finally the roof sections that had been built on the ground by skilled workmen. After constructing each section, they prepared it for being lifted by fastening chains in the exact position to balance the weight, making it possible for the crane to lift it safely to its proper position. I watched from my apartment window, as one large, perfectly-balanced section was slowly lifted, then lowered to be attached to the building walls. As the roof hung just inches above the building, four workmen, standing at corners of the existing building, gently guided it while the crane lowered it to its final position.

Now I REALLY appreciated the skill of the operator of that huge crane. From his seat in the cab he performed the delicate maneuvers of setting the roof into the exact, correct position. What a thrilling sight!

Meanwhile, another building was under construction at the end of the facing wing of the main building. From my vantage point, I watched the youngm strong workmen building *that* roof in place above the building. I marveled at their ability to maintain good balance as they worked on the sloping roof. Fortunately, they wore safety ropes, should they lose their balance.

The large basement under the two buildings is a parking garage. The first building addition has 16 lovely apartments, and the second building is a well-equipped wellness center, with a lap pool, an exercise pool, a spa, a sauna, steam rooms, massage rooms, exercise equipment, and dressing rooms.

The buildings were completed and ready for occupancy in September 2011. We had a grand celebration on the day of the dedication, with a significant meal that included roast prime rib, served in a huge tent erected in the courtyard between the two new additions.

Ongoing improvements and upgrades on our campus continue to make our lives comfortable. My early reluctance to move here has changed to thankfulness for my good fortune in making new friends with mutual interests, and experiencing the comforts provided by URC.

URC Addition - Photo by Ruth Wildman

AND DEATH SHALL HAVE NO DOMINION[28]

By Madalon Amenta

Today I was full of Moxie
loaded for bear
spitting piss and vinegar

Were my planets
maybe finally
in harmonic convergence?

Had the young person inside me
maybe stopped whining
What the hell happened?

Had the antiprostaglandins
maybe finally defeated the Albigentians
on the ancient battlefield of my body?

Who knows? Who cares?

Smashing passion filled our afternoon!

MYRNA'S REFLECTIONS[29]
An Alter Ego Poem
By Gailen Keeling

When my darling Olden died,
   my world seemed to end
For I had just lost
   my very best friend.

I grieve for my loss,
   feeling suffering and pain.
It's the price that one pays
   for all that they've gained.

Gray clouds now surround me.
Sun and moon seem so dim.
I'm oh so much missing,
   the time spent with him.

While sadness enfolds me,
   showing the loss that I feel,
I'll be sad for a season,
   then, I'll proudly reveal

The wonderful memories:
Treasures in head and in heart
For the one who so loved me,
   as I make a new start.

ECCE HOMO[30]
By Madalon Amenta

Dust and gas
Pain and ashes

We sigh
  Sometimes
  We smile

Sometimes
  We even fly
  A little

WE KNOW[31]
By Madalon Amenta

Crack of thunder
Rush of wind
Light and heat of sun
Oak leaf floating slowly to the ground
Under a full October moon

All we have is time and each other

OCTOBER 2005[32]

By Madalon Amenta

Life is an onion and one peels it crying
— French Proverb

Three times this week
   alone, puttering around the house
   with the TV on for company
I didn't just wipe away the idle tear
   I wept
   I cried
   I cried hard
   I cried so hard I surprised myself

   When Geena Davis as Mackenzie Allen
     the first woman president
     addressed a joint session of Congress

   When August Wilson who died so young
     was eulogized for
     systematically and passionately
     articulating the history
     of American blacks
     in the twentieth century

   When an old, old white bearded rabbi
     in ceremonial regalia
     was shown blowing a shofar

   And then on the phone I found out
     there'll be more grandchildren—
     twins!

I wouldn't have believed it possible

---

but I cried even harder

Soaking myself in tears
I sobbed and sobbed
   like Isaac Babel
   being dragged by the NKVD
   flailing and shrieking
   from his apartment

I'm not finished!
I'm not finished!

Living, Loving, Laughing at the Carnegie Museum, Pittsburgh PA
Photo by Michael K. Gainer

THE KISS[33]

By Madalon Amenta

"...he drew
With one long kiss, my whole soul through
My lips." – Alfred Lord Tennyson, 1833

We had spent the day prosaically. No romantic settings, no agendas, no plans – no overt ones, anyway – but to have a pleasant time and to get to know each other better. It was only the third time we had been together, and we were still being sensible. Maybe we were being cautious like the late middle-aged people we were, he a new sixty and me sixty-four and a quarter. A few weeks earlier in mid-March the worst snow storm to hit the area in a hundred years had prevented our seeing each other sooner.

While walking to a movie the second time we were together in early April, I had told him that my daughter, who was visiting from California, was going with my ex-husband and his wife to the Science Museum, something I had never done. Michael went *carpe diem* as unselfconsciously as a naïve teenager.

"I would love to take you. That's someplace in Pittsburgh that I know a lot about. I've been wondering if there was anything you'd like to do that I could take the lead in. I'll be the tour guide. How about next Saturday?"

"O.K. And I have theater tickets for that night so if you want, we can make a long day of it," I replied, smiling – not at all surprised at how easily I went along with it, at how familiar, natural, unguarded and comfortable the whole negotiation seemed.

Why would I have been surprised? I had been writing in my journal about my sense of isolation, my despair, a marrow-piercing loneliness. The Good Friday entry – "Crazy! – Hungry! – Lonely!

Got into bed early and read the book *I'm Dysfunctional; You're Dysfunctional!"*

Late night movies on TV that depicted intact families, love that lasted, loyal intimate friendships – no matter how unrealistic or icky sentimental – sent ascending paroxysmal sobs through my torso. They stopped as suddenly as they started. Catharsis accomplished? I never asked, just noted the events like a good vulcanologist.

Almost a month to the day before the Science Museum date, the journal entry read, "This a.m. on awakening and hearing on NPR about the first woman to win the Iditerod…She hugged her lead husky and cried, 'He would have died for me and I would have died for him'…I burst into the old gut-wrenching sobs. Is that what being connected is? Is the illusion the same thing? What will Michael be like? He spends evenings in his observatory – told me last night on the phone that he had great photos of Jupiter. Can I get excited about that?"

On the day of the date, he was to arrive at nine in the morning. I bounced up at seven and took fillets and a ciabatta out of the freezer for dinner. Not wanting to seem too eager to play house I just made a fresh pot of coffee instead of setting out goodies for munching. Let him take care of his own breakfast!

I dressed casually, but with great care. Classic Scottish tartan plaid skirt for that Ivy League look (serious, intelligent, well educated), white wool and angora turtleneck sweater (who wouldn't want to touch?), well-worn brown knee-high smooth calfskin boots (expensive, sure, but durable). I chose the underwear with even more care. Best engineered under-wired uplift lace bra in the drawer, satin spandex briefs, and a taffeta slip that rustled. I sprinkled Giorgio cologne under my arms and around the base of my neck.

He rang the bell right on time, refused coffee, and I threw on a duffle coat, grabbed my backpack and we were off into the crisp sunshine in his little red Ford Festiva.

During a scary moment in the IMAX simulation of John Wesley Powell's early exploratory Colorado River raft trips through the

Grand Canyon, I gasped, "Don't lose the data!" clutching the arm of the seat, being careful to only brush Michael's arm in the process. Afterward as we toured the various exhibits I occasionally brushed up against him as if by accident. When we were in the car driving to the brewery on Troy Hill for a German lunch, he clasped my knee laughing after I made a joke and said, "You're a very attractive woman, you know."

I laughed back, "Yes, I know that."

At lunch, we talked of science, art, music, politics, work, dreams. We soared higher and higher feeding each other on a trajectory of anticipated possibilities as the wursts and wieners, krauts and potatoes and beer after beer came flowing along. When thinking about dessert Michael said, "I would like to eat everything on the menu." It thrilled me.

Next we went to the Carnegie Museum in Oakland and Michael showed me his favorite natural history and science exhibits. We also looked at some new art. Although I thought he lacked sophistication and background, his reactions were open, intelligent, enthusiastic.

Suddenly, I was exhausted. We drove to my house and I put him on the third floor in one of the long-unused children's bedrooms, then drew the blinds and fell into a deep sleep in my own king-sized bed on the floor below.

For dinner we had steak, baked potatoes, artichokes with three different dips, green salad, red wine and apple pie. We ate family-style in the kitchen, I in a housecoat and apron, he in dungarees and a sweatshirt. We talked like old friends.

"I've never had artichokes before. I don't think I much like them."

"That's O.K. They're an acquired taste, like beer, and you seemed to like that well enough at lunch."

Again, his response was honest, factual, easy, no negative charge. Part of me had remained vigilant and analytical all day. I was watching for any signs of hostility, lack of confidence, withholding, or hints of meanness.

When we were finished, we left the dishes on the table and ran to our respective rooms to change for the theater. It was a play called *Temptation* by Vaclav Havel, a retelling in modern terms of the Faust legend, hardly an original or gripping plot. We were both receptive, however, because of Havel's political significance and the great sympathy in which he is held in liberal circles throughout the Western world.

The first act was dull – philosophical dialogue with next to no action. After intermission there was no change – just repetitions of the same conversations and ideas. In a few minutes, Michael was looking at me, rather than at the stage.

I looked back and he said, "Had enough?" We got up and left. Neither of us had ever walked out in the middle of a live performance before. We were in sync.

As we approached my house, I was wondering, "What do we do now?"

When he stopped the car he said, "I have to come in to pick up my clothes."

"Oh, right," said I matter-of-factly. Confirming.

Once inside he bounded up the stairs and I went into the kitchen to start cleaning up the dinner dishes. I was queasy about how things would be left. For sure, I knew I wanted continuation.

He came into the kitchen coat on, carrying his bag and extended the free arm. I threw both my arms around his shoulders, hugging him with all my strength. No observation now, no analysis, just passion and need. He did not resist, did not even stiffen slightly, but hugged me back with equal force. Then we found each other's mouths and kissed – hard, wet, messy. We clasped hands and walked into the living room, lighting on the love seat and embracing again as soon as we were able. He threw his coat off.

"I can stay the night," he said, his hand up the back of my blouse fiddling with the clasp of my bra.

"Oh, God," I muttered. "Wait a minute. Let's think about this. Who did you vote for President?"

"Clinton," in a tone that clearly meant, "Who else?"

Having been to a two-day HIV conference during the week, I asked, "Aren't you afraid I might have AIDS?"

"No, and you know I couldn't have it. I told you the only woman I've ever slept with was my wife."

"Don't you think we should wait just a little longer?"

"For what?"

"I have to clean up the kitchen."

"I can help you. I can DO it myself."

I had run out of questions and reasons. He was right. What is the point of the whole merry rigmarole? If it seems to be working, isn't the natural thing to have it end up in bed? And the day had certainly been a natural. What did either of us have to lose?

Upstairs I took a pair of pajamas (harder to get into than a nightgown) out of a drawer and went into the bathroom to put them on. I was shy about him seeing me – a woman in her 65th year, yet – naked. He got into bed while I was changing.

After I had joined him and we fondled – tenderly, lightly, tentatively exploring, he asked, "Do you like my body?"

"Why wouldn't I?"

"Because of all my operations."

His unabashed vulnerability flushed through my blood like a drug. I shimmied out of the pajamas and we embraced.

In two minutes it was over. It had been five years for him, six for me. I yelled out, "We've got passed it. We've got passed it."

He said softly, "I never thought I would hold a woman in my arms again."

The journal entries started changing. The next day I wrote, "Last night I took Michael into my home, into my body, into my soul."

Two days later, "A few weeks ago I was looking for a geriatrician, now it's a gynecologist. Amazing! Do not feel old now! To my deepest self this seems like the most natural thing in the world. It is something that SHOULD have happened, and I am excited, and calm and grateful all at the same time."

Three weeks later, "In the beginning is an ending. How far will we take each other? What a pleasure to explore. Will we go the distance? I hold this like a precious secret. I cherish it."

And people were noticing a change in me. A man, a Republican with whom I sat on a State board in Harrisburg, asked me after a not-as-biting-as-usual exchange, "Hey, what's happened to you, are you in love?"

My longest-standing friend in life who lived in Manhattan called and said my voice and manner seemed softer. I told her what was going on. She laughed and said, "Ah, so you ARE changed."

What are these things – RELATIONSHIPS? Surely mysteries. No one, least of all the people involved, can figure them out. Maybe they are cosmic and when the time is right, the right people conjoin.

The year this happened, we not only had the worst snowstorm for the date in a hundred years, but the magnolias came to full bloom, a thing we didn't often see in Pittsburgh. The tree outside my bedroom window became effulgent and a poem came to me, a thing that hadn't happened for forty five years.

MID-APRIL – GRAY

First magnolia buds outside the bedroom window
Sparse, tight, purple veined, tentative
Prick of frost – they stiffen into brown cones
Then fall away.
    It almost always happens
    Will one never not be alone?
    This year the magnolias blossom!
Cumulus, billowing
White to pink to fuchsia to plum.

Red joy rides down the street.

156

AN UNEXPECTED ANGEL[34]

By Carol Gass

On Christmas Day 2010, our daughter Katrina and I were washing up some dishes. My husband Michael came into the kitchen reading aloud from a pamphlet on "stress management" that had come to us from our health insurance provider's Wellness Program. The section that caught his eye was about how pets are good stress reducers.

He is always so thoughtful and knows that I have a continuous level of stress related to our daughter Pam's on-going serious health issues. I do everything I can to relieve stress: exercise, good diet, wonderful loving support from family and friends, easy sharing and tears as they come.

Michael inherited not only three more daughters when he married me twenty-six and a half years ago, he also inherited a young dog and cat, both of whom lived to be almost seventeen!

He suggested on that Christmas Day that he would like to give me a dog for my gift. Of course, I was thrilled at the thought as I had always been an animal lover. Growing up, our dog, Cindy, loved all four of us kids, but I was the one who groomed her, fed her, and taught her tricks, and she and the cat both slept on my bed.

Michael grew up in India, in the village of Baitalpur, located in the center of the country, where his dad was the superintendent of a large leprosy hospital. They did have a dog, but it was mostly an outside playmate. Starting at age seven, he was at Kodaicanal International School, a boarding school in South India and away from home much of the year.

In answer to Michael's proposal about getting a dog, I said that I loved the idea, but that we needed to be totally honest with each other in this decision. I didn't want my stress level to go down and his up. After our previous pets died, we had agreed that we wouldn't

---

[34] Copyright©2914 Carol Gass

get more. We discussed the idea over several days, and by Wednesday after Christmas, a decision had been made.

If we could find a small dog, non-shedding, with a calm demeanor, that was not a yapper, we would adopt one. That was quite a list for any little dog to live up to. Our local daughter Wendy, also an animal lover, was right on it. She went online and by the next day found a little dog in Vacaville for us to visit. It was a cute little dog, but too hyper for us.

On Friday Wendy found another one for us to check out. It was New Year's Eve, and she, Michael and I and the two grandchildren, Hailey (14) and Christopher (11), piled into their van, and off we went to Elk Grove to an SPCA facility. It was a drizzly afternoon when we arrived at this kennel in the country. People from the city boarded their dogs at this facility due to the New Year's Eve fireworks in town. The boarders were in the back and the SPCA dogs in a large room with multiple wire enclosures containing many dogs of similar size.

We took the one we had come to see for a walk outside and almost were ready to sign the papers when he sprayed my leg. There was no way we were going to bring that dog home.

I asked the owner what she had in the way of a small female. She went into the back, brought out a little white Maltese/Poodle mix and put her into the enclosure right by me. She stood up on her back legs, wagging her tail and looking adorable. I picked her up, and we all went outside to walk her around. The rain picked up, so we got into the van and passed her around lap to lap. She was so calm and just settled down happily into each lap.

We went back in and learned a little of her history. She was turned into the Stockton city pound on Christmas Eve after obviously being on the streets for some time. They showed us a picture of her taken the day she was turned in to the pound. She was very thin with long matted hair over her eyes. Stockton kept her several days and then sent her to the Elk Grove SPCA rescue where they clipped her hair very short due to the matting. She weighed all of 8½ pounds.

We promised to have her spayed by our veterinarian in Davis and soon were on our way home with our sweet little girl. We had to decide on a suitable name. Lots of ideas were tossed around. Finally, with input from everyone, especially the kids, we decided on Kali Talullahbelle Shanti Gass. Of course we would call her Kali.

On the way home we stopped at Petco and bought a bed, dishes, food, a toy, a name tag with our phone number, and a sweater. On arrival home our granddaughter Hailey and I headed right to the bathtub and got her cleaned up while the rest of the family ordered pizza. After dinner the rest of the family went home.

Michael and I sat across the room from each other and called her back and forth. She would run between us and hop right into our lap. For a brief moment we thought she shouldn't be on the furniture. Then we said, "Well, if she is on our lap, that is ok," and then about two minutes later, the decision was that Kali could be wherever she wanted!

That first night, I felt like a new mother with a baby just home. I put her little bed right by our bed and fully expected to get up with her that night. She slept quietly all night and has done so ever since. But nowadays she sleeps with us!

Kali loves everyone. She is so gentle with little children; they can pull her tail and put their fingers in her mouth – no problem. She is also a natural therapy dog and brings comfort to those in Skilled Nursing, putting her paws up on a wheelchair to be petted or hopping up on a bed when invited. People then share their own dog stories. She spreads joy everywhere we go.

 As for the two of us, I can guarantee that she is good for our health. Michael is "head over heels" in love with a dog for the first time. And, of course, I, too, am in love with our "unexpected angel" who brings so much joy to our lives,. A wonderful Christmas surprise!

Kali   *Photo by Dan Brown*

A LETTER TO ANN

By Alouise Hillier

Dear Ann,

I have some precious thoughts to add to your book of memories. They come to me in bits and pieces.

I'm remembering an extremely uncomfortable pregnancy during the miserable, 100-plus temperature in Stillwater, Oklahoma, where Dad attended summer school, pursuing a doctoral degree. Lynn, Susan and I often accompanied Dad to the air-conditioned library. He studied and researched, the girls watched TV, and I sat on a couch in the library and slept.

The heat spell continued after our return to Pittsburg. We had no air conditioning there either. I remember lying on the bed in the back bedroom with a fan and the windows open for fresh air, trying to find some relief. One day I overheard Lynn tell her neighborhood playmate that she couldn't play because she had work to do. The friend said, "My mother doesn't make me work!!" Lynn replied, "My mother is sick, and I have to help her." This from an 8-year-old! How could I have expected so much from her?

On Labor Day, September 1, 1952, we had the great surprise and thrill of having you arrive, followed by your sister a few minutes later. Dad, sitting in the waiting room, in his joking manner assured the new student nurses that he was confident this would be a son. After your arrival, they gleefully told him that he had a girl, and then even more gleefully they came back a few minutes later to tell him that he had another girl. We had had no idea we were having twins!

Because children could not visit in the hospital, Dad brought Lynn and Susan to the side of the building where they could look up to the second floor to see me standing at the window holding the two of you.

161

9/7/52

Grandma Hillier had planned to come, but she was taken ill, so we had no one at home to help us. I stayed in the hospital for two weeks, paid for by our health insurance. The inactivity during that long stay bored me, but I knew that would change drastically after our discharge from the hospital.

When we brought you home, all the neighborhood children came trouping in, one or two at a time, to see you. You looked so much alike that at first I kept the hospital bracelets on you for fear I would mix you up. Later, as toddlers, I could identify you by the cowlick above your forehead.

We had chosen the name Ann Martha for a girl, but weren't prepared with another girl's name, so Lynn and Susan helped in planning the second name. A teen-aged girl named Ruth had lived in our neighborhood in Vet Village in Stillwater. Lynn and Susan loved her and wanted to name the baby Ruth. Lynn had read the book *Robinhood* and really liked Maid Marian, so she chose that for Ruth's second name. You were named for Aunt Ann and Grandmother Martha. Aunt Marian always thought Ruth was named for her, but we didn't ever tell her that was not really the case.

Happy and contented babies, you quickly learned that you would be picked up for cuddling and play when the girls and Dad came in from school. You started calling "Eh heh, eh heh" as soon as you heard their footsteps on the front porch.

162

One memorable day, Dad came home to take care of you so that I could get away for a short while. When I returned, the door was blocked, because you had picked up and carried the playpen to the wall so that it blocked the door. Daddy was taking a nap! I was REALLY mad at him! You had played your favorite game of "break the bottle," too! Dad suddenly realized that life was not simply "give the babies their bottles, put them in the play pen, and take a nap!" Luckily, you weren't cut badly, only minor scratches on your hands.

You loved to break bottles! Each day after putting you to bed with your bottle, you somehow broke them after emptying them. One day, Lynn, Susan, Dad and I peeped in to see you aim and throw your bottle at a short metal pipe in the floor. What a good aim! You both should have been baseball pitchers! You also entertained each other by taking turns performing bounces or jumps to make your twin laugh.

One day when I was cleaning house, I became aware of an unusually suspicious silence. I hastily went in search of you two. In the kitchen, you had opened the refrigerator door, pulled out a dozen eggs, broken and scrambled them on the floor. You seemed intent on getting the top off a ketchup bottle, no doubt with the intention of adding that to the mix.

Ruth   Ann

The TV program "Captain Kangaroo" seemed a lifesaver to me. You sat quietly to watch it, thus giving me some rest time. You really were good girls – just so curious and interested in everything that you kept us hopping. You had some mischief in you, also. You loved to tease me by walking on the piano keys when I talked on the phone with my friend. No cordless phones in those days, so you were just beyond my reach. We lovingly called you "The Terrible Two!"

163

I made most of our clothes, including coats for you. I didn't stress dressing you alike, but could make two of the same fabric most economically. By placing the pattern pieces carefully I wasted less material. Most of the time, you chose to wear different dresses, but sometimes you decided to be "twins today" and dressed alike.

It amused Dad to remember your learning to read. One day when you encountered a word you didn't know, you said you didn't know it – "that's Ruth's word." You had the same teachers for kindergarten and first grade, but then until sixth grade had different teachers. At the urging of your classmates, you sometimes exchanged seats to confuse the first male teacher you had.

You paid me such a lovely compliment when you told me that you were proud of me because I didn't gossip. You often left loving notes to me on my pillow – sometimes apologies, but mostly expressions of love.

I am proud of your skill and devotion to your students. These students will always remember you as a very special teacher in their lives. I know you were sorely missed when you were compelled to retire. Now your sweet patience is an inspiration to everyone who comes into contact with you. I'm sure the other MS patients whom you contact and inspire are thankful for your cheerfulness. Dad would say, "You are a good kid!"

I LOVE YOU,
Mother

BEING MORTAL – A Book Review

By Joan Callaway

Over the past several weeks, Elli Norris and I have facilitated a group discussion of advanced end-of-life planning – a topic Dr. Atul Gawande, an oncologist, covers extensively in his new book, *Being Mortal: Medicine and What Matters in the End.* Intended for a general audience, this book is a good addition to the national debate about end-of-life issues. With many concrete examples from his practice and his family, he provides a thoughtful assessment of the many economic, political and social concerns that stand in the way of supporting individuals who wish to live productively in their aging, but hope for, in the end, a good death.

He takes on the question that everyone faces: How can we make our last days more comfortable, meaningful, and affordable? Sophisticated medical care does not guarantee and often actually prevents a good end of life. What comes through most clearly is the importance of avoiding the inevitable. To die a good death means finding, in life, the courage to have caring and frequent conversations with doctors and family about one's wishes.

Our EOL group discussions at University Retirement Community in Davis followed the questions in the American Bar Association's *Consumer's Toolkit for Health Care Advance Planning* (www.americanbar.org). Our discussions focused on how we wish to be ensured comfort, care and respect during our last moments. Dr. Gawande urges these kinds of discussions prior to the imminent need, as he says that far too often patients are in such denial of their imminent deaths that they, or their families, demand futile life-saving measures. He criticizes doctors, himself included, for their inability to confront the fact of death that often prevents them from counseling patients wisely. The most important question a doctor can ask, according to Dr. Gawande, is "If time becomes short, what is most important to you?"

Dr. Gawande's masterful exploration of aging, death, and the medical profession's mishandling of both is a little depressing – until you get to the parakeets! He introduces us to Bill Thomas, who redesigned a New York nursing home, planting gardens for residents to tend and an on-site day-care center so they could interact with children. And brought in 100 parakeets – and birdsong. The results are encouraging.

DUC – THE STORY
By Joan Callaway

Everyone at University Retirement Community in Davis has a **Duc Nguyen** story about how he has helped them during his thirteen years as master problem solver of the Facilities Department. This story, however, takes us back to 1974 when, as a 2nd Lieutenant and an artillery platoon leader in the Vietnamese Marine Corps, he was chosen for intensive study of English. As a high scorer, he was one of four officers selected to gain further training at Marine University at Quantico, Va. When that training was complete, they warned him not to go back to Vietnam, but he said, "It is my home. I have family. It is my country."

Upon his return home in 1975, shortly after Communist forces broke the 1973 Peace Accord and captured Saigon, he was arrested along with his fellow officers, and incarcerated in unbelievable conditions for six long years. Closely guarded, they worked in hot fields by day – "over eight hours a day with no shoes, no hat, and not enough water." At night they lay on concrete floors, side-by-side, shackled to each other by one leg. They received one level bowl of rice three times a day. "That's all." Literally starving, they scavenged every living thing they could find – scorpions, centipedes, all kinds of insects, and, yes, "cobra? – mmm, delicious, more than happy!"

After his release in 1981, he attended Polytechnic University-Saigon, as well as learned about air conditioning and refrigeration under the tutelage of an uncle. His father, a Marine Corps Colonel, advised him, "Son, remember, if anyone can do it, you can do it."

During the next six years in which he accumulated enough money to apply for refugee status, he gained invaluable experience repairing washers, dryers, and refrigerators in Saigon. "It took many papers. For every paper and at every turn, I had to pay – much money." With refugee status eventually confirmed, he came to the

United States in 1994 with his wife An and their two-year old daughter. He went back to school and studied for his citizenship, while receiving an AS degree in mechanical electrical technology.

That daughter, Phuong, now 22, is a senior, majoring in biology at UC Davis. A son Nam, born in 1995 at Mercy Hospital in Sacramento, is in his second year at Sacramento State University studying mechanical engineering. With two children in college and a 16-month-old granddaughter Nhi, this year's EAF* (Employee Appreciation Fund) gift will be more than appreciated.

*Published in *URCADIAN*. November 2014

Phuong, Nam, An, and Duc Nguyen

*Employees at URC are not permitted to accept gratuities for their service, so in an attempt to show appreciation residents may contribute to a fund during the year or during a fund drive. The EAF fund is distributed at a party early in December to those employees on the payroll on December 1ˢᵗ, based on the number of hours they have worked during the year.

WHEN THINGS CHANGED

By Joan Callaway

One day a few years ago as my son-in-law drove me, my daughter, and my grandson and his girlfriend of one year home from a water polo game in Lodi, he commented that he was sorry that the young couple hadn't met when they were in their late 20's; they are so companionable and compatible. Both had plans for college – my grandson had already been accepted at the Air Force Academy in Colorado Springs; his girlfriend hoped to go to the University of Oregon. In any case, not in the same direction!

I couldn't help but recall my own graduation from Lincoln High School in Tacoma, Washington, just sixty years ago, bright eyed and looking forward to majoring in journalism at the University of Washington in Seattle, while my boyfriend of two years was headed to Reed College in Portland, Oregon. Whether it was a strict sense of morality or fear of pregnancy, I cannot say, but we had restrained our sexual urges as had most of our friends. We had every intention of continuing the relationship beyond our college years, believing that one day we would marry.

But first, for me it was my math expertise that garnered me a job for the summer as a beginning actuary at an insurance company in Seattle at $140 a month, while for Glen it was his brawn and past experience that got him a contract with the U. S. Forestry Service to remove rust-producing *ribes Americanum* (commonly called black currant, a member of the gooseberry family) from the white pine forests of Idaho – $4,000 for the summer – already obvious disparity of income-producing opportunities.

The summer ended, and while I lived at home with my mother and attended classes at the University of Washington, Glen, with a full scholarship to Reed College, lived in a dorm-like house off campus, working as a short-order cook at a nearby cafe.

I made an occasional weekend trip to Portland, sometimes staying at one of the women's dorms or occasionally at a local hotel. In spite

169

of widening opportunities, we never violated our parents' trust or our own sense of "not until we are married." Again, I'm not sure how much fear of pregnancy entered into the picture, as by this time a few friends had "had to get married." Both of us wanted college first. Discontented with introductory courses at the U of W, I transferred to Reed the next September.

It became more and more difficult to say goodnight at the door of Kerr Hall especially with Smitty, the night watchman, standing patiently nearby, so we soon decided to ask my parents if they would continue to pay my tuition and equivalent board and room if we got married. When they agreed, we planned a small wedding in Vancouver immediately after the semester ended, with a short honeymoon to follow at a small seaside town cottage.

We returned to live upstairs over the infirmary, changing beds and cleaning up after patients our only chores. This provided us a small income plus board and room. We ate with all the students in the Commons, went to classes as usual, and could now enjoy all the pleasures of marriage. It soon became apparent that we had been wise to wait, as I soon had flu symptoms, gagged at the smell of the Lysol we used to wipe down beds after patients, and couldn't keep down greasy Commons food.

It seems that in spite of using the birth control method available to us, a diaphragm, I had gotten pregnant – ill-timed, as we had no money, were in just the second year of college, and had no prospects of careers. But we and all of our friends were overjoyed once we got over the shock.

I suspect that given similar circumstances, today's young couple would have – but no, wait! So much has changed. When did things change? I think it was shortly after my last child was born: the birth control pill, a synthetic hormone that prevents ovulation, was introduced to the public in the early 1960's. No longer did the fear of pregnancy preclude an active sex life for the married or unmarried.

170

This quiet event – the introduction of the oral contraceptive, or The Pill, as it became known – changed everything. There has been a genuine "revolution" in social attitudes. Without a shot being fired!

Sixty years ago when I graduated from high school, women had the choice of career (nurse, teacher or secretary mostly) or housework and child care. Today women can hold almost any job they want. It wasn't The Pill alone, but it was the punctuation mark to Women's Liberation that had been trudging along since the 40's.

Because every hand had been needed for the war effort during World War II, women and colored people were offered a wider range of opportunities in the work place than ever before. This was when women began to wear pants and occasionally the pants in the family. Once the war ended, however, those in power tried to restore society to how it had been – with women in the kitchen. Women who did have jobs outside the home were relegated to dead-end jobs and were paid far less than men for the same job. (That has not changed much; women still complain of being paid less than men.)

The Pill, the first reliable means of contraception, gave women the power to plan or avoid pregnancies. The Civil Rights movement forced the passage of Title VII of the Civil Rights Act of 1964, which forbade job discrimination on the basis of race, color, religion, sex or national origin.

I laugh out loud as I watch the young, newly-promoted ad copy writer in *Mad Men* assert her rights, refuse to fetch the coffee, or demand that she get pay equal to that of her male counterpart when it is she who had had the original idea. You can tell by this early-60's-based TV show that the AIDS epidemic had not yet come into the consciousness as both men and women seem quite sexually liberated.

Since the late 1960's, amniocentesis and ultrasound have become very common obstetrical procedures, used not only for genetic evaluation, but also for diagnosing fetal maturity and other issues. The ability to plan or avoid pregnancy with The Pill had not been enough. Now doctors could determine sex of fetus and any genetic defects.

171

Couples could worry for the remainder of the pregnancy about problems yet to come.

Assuming that a woman no longer had to have accidental pregnancies, what of those women impregnated through rape or incest or in the case of danger to the mother's health or an obvious defect in the fetuUntil this time, abortion had been legal in some states, but not in others. Back alley abortions, often in unsterile conditions, as well as self-induced ones, often led to unfortunate outcomes. With this new information available, it seemed logical that the next step would be legalization of abortion, the "woman's right to choose" what happens to her body.

The Roe v. Wade Supreme Court decision of January 1973 held that a woman, with her doctor, could choose abortion in the earlier months of pregnancy without restriction, and with restrictions in later months, based on a woman's constitutional right to privacy.

§§§

I finished out the year after Glen and I married, but made no college plans for the fall as our baby was due in late November of 1951. I would be a stay-at-home mom, a term that had not yet been coined. We would have a baby, sex as yet unknown. No pill, no ultrasound, no amniocentesis, and no thought of abortion.

Our baby surprised us though and was born six weeks earlier than expected, to all eyes perfect in every way. A girl! 5# 5 oz. She had the softest, most velvety skin. Little did we know then, but that velvety skin was indicative of a birth defect. The first time she fell down after she started walking, she got a laceration – not a scraped knee – a laceration requiring stitches.

It wasn't diagnosed – though there were many such trips to the E.R. – until she was nearly six. She had Ehlers-Danlos syndrome, a collagen disease. I assume amniocentesis would have discovered this had they been doing it back in 1951, although my pregnancy was normal throughout, unless you call that little bout of morning sickness abnormal.

I'm glad, however, that we didn't have all those medical advantages; I'm glad we didn't have to make that choice. And knowing what I know now, I'm glad I didn't *plan* my pregnancies around a career choice or around what amniocentesis might have shown.

In spite of her medical challenges of scoliosis, frequent suture requirements, as well as dislocations, when Valerie began thinking of having her own children, she and her husband went for genetic counseling. They were told they had a fifty-fifty chance of having a child with Ehlers-Danlos syndrome. As it turns out, one of her two children does have the syndrome. Neither she nor I would make a different choice.

There are lessons to be learned from having a special needs child – for the parents, the child, and the siblings. For myself, I wouldn't change the several months that Valerie as a teenager had to spend in a full-body cast in a hospital bed in her bedroom at home, as that was a most precious time – a rare special time that we both remember.

If I had known ahead of time, might I have made a different choice? Had she been diagnosed earlier, might I have elected not to have had further pregnancies? Oh, how sad that would have been! None of my other four children have the syndrome.

Having more choices – the birth control pill, legalized abortion, and more technology on which to base those choices – is this progress we can believe in?

§§§

In just sixty years, we have gone from abstinence until marriage the norm to "in a relationship" and "hooking up" casual sex announced on Facebook and Twitter by high school and college age students. No stigma, no deep emotional involvement, or so it would appear. I guess it must mean some emotional involvement when someone posts "In a relationship" on their Facebook profile. I'm still not quite sure - perhaps what we used to mean by "Going steady?" Or does it imply more? Is this change we can believe in?

The Brady Bunch iconic family of mom, dad and the kids all living under one roof is dwindling. The number of unmarried couples, as well as childless couples and single person households, is increasing.

Marriage among college graduates has become much more selective. And that probably accounts for the divorce rate in the United States slowly declining since its peak in the late 1970's. Divorce rate for college graduates is only a third as high as for those with just high school degree.

However, now more and more often couples are cohabiting instead of marrying, and those breakups are not included in the statistics. Marriage comes later, if at all.

Sperm donors make alternative families possible for women who choose not to marry, but still want to have a family; an unmarried woman, lesbian or not, can – with little or no stigma – choose this method of having a child. This is definitely a big change.

My parents loved me and wanted me to be happy. I loved my children and wanted them to be happy, too. And there's no question that they also want that for their children. The difference between the generations lies in parenting styles, new approved methods, and the quality of monitoring.

I had a nanny most of my early childhood, because unlike the mothers of most of my friends, my mother did work outside the home. Today, with an economy and a desire of a certain middle class life style two incomes are often required. The cell phone and texting have replaced the after-school chat with cookies and milk that children of earlier generations enjoyed. Dr Spock was the childrearing bible of my era. Today book stores have a whole section on the different kinds of parenting.

Instead of the "good enough" parents, everyone hopes to not make the mistakes their parents made, sometimes perhaps even overdoing the "being attuned" to their child's every need, as with the "helicopter mom's" hovering. In this era, it seems that to assure a child's happiness, the current trend is child-centered with parents often running themselves ragged driving their child to and from school, music lessons, gymnastics, and dance lessons, as well as attending every game and every school event – or feeling guilty when they can't. Blogs on-line tell of parents' anxiety and their empty-nest syndrome as they try to adjust to their own life when their last child leaves for college. Everyone hopes for their children to be happy.

Alas! Happiness is an elusive thing. It cannot be bestowed. Some things never change.

ACKNOWLEDGMENTS

Not long after my husband and I moved into our Garden Apartment at University Retirement Community, we began getting invitations to have dinner with residents who had been here for some time. I heard their voices, like mine, longing to share their stories – but so fleetingly. I yearned for those stories to be written down for posterity.

I had seen the value of putting to paper our memories. Value not just for our families, but for the clarification that comes during the writing of our stories. I had been a part of a legacy writing group for several year, which led to the publishing of my own memoir, *It's an Ill Wind, Indeed,* and a true legacy book, *Invisible to the Eye.- The First Forty Years.* I had experienced the magic.

Almost as soon as the boxes were unpacked, at the urging of friends I gave a reading from those books, and from that grew the idea of a memoir/legacy writing group at URC Davis.

Over the past year and a half, the voices of that group, hungry for telling the truth, and courageous in their sharing, have given me a year-long gift – and now to you, the reader, in this end-of-year 'recital.'

Here are some of the voices of people who have sustained me: Pat Hutchinson, one of the writers who had participated in the writing group at my home for several years and who urged me to begin such a group at URC; Lena Mc Nicholas, author of *Patchwork: Pieces of Appalachia,* who from time to time visited the group, sharing her ideas on memoir in free verse; and, of course, all the authors of the pieces you will find in this book; but first and foremost, my husband Ed Callaway, who encourages me to be who I must be, do what I must do.

BIOGRAPHIES

MADALON AMENTA was the Poetry Editor of both her high school (Dorchester High School for Girls) and college (Tufts) literary publications. As a young graduate she acted in productions of the Provincetown Playhouse and Circle in the Square in New York City, and Poets' Theater in Cambridge, MA. Later as a nurse she published several clinical and academic papers, manuals, newsletters, research reports and books, one of which won an American Journal of Nursing Book of the Year Award. In retirement she returned to poetry and her work has appeared in journals and anthologies such as *Salon.com*, *Pittsburgh City Paper*, *Pittsburgh Post Gazette* and *Voices from the Attic*. Her chapbook, *Kandinsky and the Stars*, published in 2010 by Finishing Line Press, was a finalist in both the Negative Capability Press International and the Blue Light Press Chapbook Competitions. At URC she enjoys writing for the URCADIAN and participating in the Memoir writing group. [pp. 145, 147, 151, 156]

CAROL GASS was born and raised in Berkeley, California. She graduated from UC Berkeley with a Bachelor of Arts degree. Later she got her nursing degree from Arapahoe Community College in Denver.

She has three daughters, three step-daughters, six grandchildren and an amazing husband Michael. She worked for over 20 years at Sutter Davis Hospital, primarily in the Surgery Center. Her special interests include family, gardening and social justice issues. "I'm especially thankful to live at URC in Davis, an exceptional town." [pp. 157]

ALOUISE HILLIER was born and grew up in the small North Dakota town of Kindred. Almost as she stepped off the train on her first day of college in Mayville, N. D., she met a fellow student who would one day be her husband. They married after his graduation and enlistment during World War II. Following the war, they proceeded to move from North Dakota to Minnesota to Kansas to Oklahoma, as he worked on a doctorate while teaching full time. When they finally settled long term in New Mexico, while raising four daughters and a son, Alouise went back to school to complete a degree in elementary education, after which she taught remedial reading for 15 years. Finally. as her husband's health declined. they moved to Davis and URC to be near their daughters. There she pursued her interest in sewing by constructing quilts that won many regional prizes. Presently she is enthusiastically engaged in the URC Memoirs group.[pp. 13, 135, 139, 141, 161]

GAILEN KEELING was born in Kansas the youngest of four children He attended public schools in Witchita and excelled in athletics – baseball, football and basketball – and graduated in the top ten of his class. He attended Kansas Wesleyan University before applying for a scholarship to New York University School of Law for his first year, followed by Washburn University School of Law. After graduation, facing threat of being drafted into the Korean conflict, he joined the Navy JAG Corps, where he served two years as the Legal Office on an aircraft carrier and his final two years at the Pentagon doing Appellate Review of Court Martial cases. At the age of 29, he was admitted to the Supreme Court. He served as an Assistant City Attorney, a Trust Officer for a National Bank, and practiced law. He graduated from Central Baptist Seminary in Kansas City. He and two colleagues established Mid-Valley Counseling Center. After his wife died, he moved to University Retirement Center in semi-retirement, and since writing had been a hobby for many years, joined the Memoir Writing group when it was offered. [pp. 5, 15, 39, 43, 44, 47, 50, 52, 54, 56, 58, 61, 146]

NANCY MAYNARD was born in San Francisco and raised in Millbrae, California.. She attended Mount Zion Hospital School of Nursing in San Francisco, from which her mother and aunt had graduated. Later she went to California State University, Chico for her baccalaureate and the University of Wisconsin, Milwaukee for her masters. She worked in Pediatrics, Public Health and the last 16 years of her career teaching at Alverno College in Milwaukee."It was my teaching career that gave me the most satisfaction, as I watched young women at this women's college mature and embark on their careers in nursing, knowing I played a part in that. After living in Wisconsin for 43 years, I wanted to come home to California, so moved to the University Retirement Community in Davis in 2013." [pp. 35, 91, 119]

ELLI NORRIS was born and raised in Porterville, Tulare County, California. "I fled "for life" after high school, wore various work hats – journalist, student, research psychologist, family therapist, and, best of all, rancher and land steward. That hat came to me after I inherited the family ranch in the foothills of the Southern Sierra after my mother's death in 1991. I went home in search of myself and with the goal of preserving the land as open space forever. As I had hoped, the land is now preserved 'in perpetuity,' and is owned by the Tulare County Office of Education for use in their outdoor education program."

She told herself when she was in high school, "When I grow up I'll be a writer." Her main writing "discipline" is journaling, which she does most days. "Sometimes it's just telling myself what I've done that day. Other times it's my way of exploring life's mysterious ways, and where I fit in them. Still, do I claim to be a *writer*?" [pp.11, 104,122, 123, 129]

DEBORAH NICHOLS POULOS was born May 6, 1945, in Berkeley, CA. "My father, a physical chemist, had worked at the National Radiation Lab there during the war. The German generals surrendered to Eisenhower the next day, and on May 8th VE Day, or Victory in Europe Day, was declared. My parents joked, 'When Debbie was born the Germans surrendered.'"

With the war over, her family moved back to San Diego where her father was a chemistry professor at San Diego State. Just before her junior year of high school, her father was appointed the founding president of Sonoma State College, so they moved to Santa Rosa where she finished high school. She went on to UC Davis where she received a B.A. in English and her elementary teaching credential. She taught elementary school for 27 years, mostly in Davis, CA. She retired in 2000 due to a progressive degenerative neuromuscular illness.

She has lived in Davis for over 40 years. From 1984-88 she served on the Davis City Council. For several years she was president of the Davis Teachers Association, and served as co-chair of a Crisis Team when the PTA was at an impasse with the school district. In 1981 she was the designer/general contractor of her own house in Village Homes when she was a single mom of her kids, Matt and Kelly, who were 8 and 6.

In 1985 she married John W. Poulos, a professor of law at UCD King Hall. "John and I have lived at University Retirement Community since 2011. Between us we have 4 kids and 13 grandkids ages 1 month to 21 years." [pp. 65, 73, 89]

JAN SMYTH spent her early years in Seattle and on Vashon Island, Washington. She attended the University of Washington, and after moving to California, graduated from Cal. State University, San Francisco. She taught for a few years, then stayed home after her sons were born. She received an M.A. from Cal State, Sonoma, with a major in counseling/ psychology. She was a counselor and taught psychology at Mendocino College in Ukiah for twenty-three years.

After Jan retired, she and her husband moved to the Monterey Peninsula, where they were docents at the Monterey Art Museum, active in the American Association of University Women, Westerners, a historical society, and their churches. Jan also learned to quilt and is currently finishing a twin size quilt.

Jan and her husband moved to University Retirement Community in Davis in 2013. They're now closer to all their children and grandchildren, and are enjoying some of the many activities offered at URC. Jan participates in Memoir/Legacy Writing and the Open Book Group, as well as serving on committees. Other interests include keeping up on national and world affairs, and finance. [105, 109, 113]

JUDY WYDICK was born and raised in rural central Missouri (Bagnell Dam, Lake of the Ozarks). She received a BS in Education and MA in English from the U. of Missouri and taught high school English in the San Francisco Bay Area from 1960-62. Since 1971, she and her husband Dick have lived in Davis, where she was deeply involved in University Farm Circle, the Pence Art Gallery, and International House-Davis. She most recently chaired the Davis Community Awards Committee. From 1992-94 she served on the California State Board of Food and Agriculture. She has written three books used as fund raisers: for the Davis High School PTA (*Preparing for College*), for high school music scholarships (*Mad[rigal] Capers*), and for UCD scholarships (*The History of University Farm Circle*). With her family she spent sabbatical years in New Zealand (1977-78), England (1987-88, 1994-95 and 2001-02), and Mallorca (2002). She and Dick (who taught at the UC Davis law school from 1971-2003) have two sons—Bruce, an economics professor at the U. of San Francisco, and Derrick, coordinator of the disabilities program at Sac City—who have provided them with granddaughters ages 5, 10 and 11. [pp.7, 21, 25, 29, 101]

ABOUT THE AUTHOR

JOAN CALLAWAY, Facilitator of the URC Memoir/Legacy Writing Group, was born and raised until the age of ten on a small farm in the State of Washington. A high school journalism class taught by an inspiring teacher led to her life-long interest in writing. Widowed at the age of forty, she went on to open two women's clothing stores, which led to the writing of her first book, *The Color Connection...from a Retailer's Perspective.* After retirement, she joined a memoir writing group and began an autobiography, but the story, *It's an Ill Wind, Indeeed,* demanded to be told before she could go on with *Invisible to the Eye – The First Forty Years.* While writing those books, she for several years participated in a memoir writing group before moving to University Retirement Community in Davis, California, with her husband, Ed. [3, 165, 167, 169, 177]

URC Memoir/Legacy Writing Group: L to R Jan Smyth, Madalon Amenta, Debbie Poulos, Elli Norris, Judy Wydick, Nancy Maynard, Alouise Hillier, and Facilitator Joan Callaway.